THE ULTIMATE FREEZE CANDY COOKBOOK

30+ Sweet Alchemy for Nurturing Bonds Through Freeze-Dried Bliss.

ABBY JARVIS

Disclaimer

Acknowledgement

Writing "THE ULTIMATE FREEZE CANDY COOKBOOK" has been a passion project for me, and I am incredibly grateful to everyone who helped make this happen.

First and foremost, I would want to thank my family, who are the source of inspiration for all the delicious recipes included inside these pages. This book has been a true labor of love because of your constant support and willingness to be taste-testers extraordinaire.

Thank you to all of my friends and neighbors, especially Mrs. Emily, whose enchanted candies inspired this project in the first place. I appreciate you sharing your happiness and gastronomic knowledge.

I want to express my appreciation to the hardworking staff at **Genesis Press** for all of their help, support, and dedication in making this project a reality. Your enthusiasm and knowledge have really
Qhelped to make this book a reality.

A special thanks to the community of freeze-dryers, whose inventiveness and dedication never cease to amaze. The information you have supplied has been very helpful in improving the recipe for freeze-dried candies.

Finally, I would like to wish all of the readers and candy lovers who take on this delicious journey a kitchen full of love, laughter, and the wonderful smells of freeze-dried enchantment.

I appreciate you traveling with me on this trip. I wish you many "Sweet Moments" and enduringly sweet relationships.

With sincere gratitude,
ABBY JARVIS.

Table of Content

Introduction

Hello, sugar seekers! Join me on an extraordinary journey into the icy realms of freeze candy, where each page promises a frosty explosion of flavor and fun. The adventure all started with a woman named Emily living in a charming neighborhood tucked between busy streets and tall buildings. Emily was a committed professional who gave her all to her work and was really passionate about it. But even with her hectic schedule, she was having to deal with an unanticipated problem her children were becoming more and more distant from her.

Emily heard her children happily speaking with Mrs. Thompson, their next-door neighbor, one seemingly normal afternoon. The children were raving about Mrs. Thompson's delicious candies and warm cookies, which stood in stark contrast to their mother's busy schedule. Emily felt a twinge of reality as she longed to close the distance and make enduring memories with her kids.

Emily started a touching adventure, determined to recover the love and laughter. She found a world of freeze-dried candy to be enchanting, a place where creativity and sweetness collided, and hectic schedules became chances for human interaction. Emily not only reignited the spark with her children but also uncovered a passion for creating delectable freeze-dried confections through fantastical stories of candy-making exploits.

"Sweet Moments" is a diary of love and intentionality rather than just a cookbook. Here are a few ideas for delicious, healthful freeze-dried candies that go above and beyond the norm. Every recipe showcases the power of love and the joy that comes with creating beautiful moments, from gummy bears that dance on your taste senses to chocolate-covered wonders that melt hearts.

This book is a tribute to people who, like Emily, are enmeshed in the chaos of their hectic schedules. It serves as a reminder that despite deadlines and responsibilities, there are a wealth of chances to forge lasting connections, fortify existing ones, and make unforgettable memories.

As you scroll through these pages, you'll find not just recipes but also hidden gems: tales of friends becoming closer with each sugary taste, of coworkers laughing over a shared bag of homemade treats, and of families united by the simple act of creating candies.

Enter the realm of "Sweet Moments," where each cuisine serves as a chapter from a love story. With each delightful creation, you can open a new chapter of love and witness the joy of sharing these delicious freeze-dried candies with your friends, family, and coworkers. Accept the adventure, relish the tastes, and let the laughter of special times to turn into the most treasured lifelong memories.

FREEZE-DRIED CANDY: WHAT IS IT?

Candy that has undergone the freeze-drying method, which involves first freezing the candy and then subjecting it to a high vacuum to sublimate the ice into vapor, is known as freeze-dried candy. Similar to what might occur in space!

IRRESISTIBLE BENEFITS OF FREEZE-DRY CANDY

1. **Intense Flavor:** The candy's natural flavors are preserved through freeze-drying, giving it a more concentrated and strong flavor. The method offers a flavor explosion with each mouthful by eliminating the water content without sacrificing flavor.

2. **Mouthfeel:** Freeze-dried candies typically have an airy, light texture that gives them a delightful crunch. This distinct texture sets the candy apart from conventionally produced sweets and adds a fun aspect to the eating experience.

3. **Increased Shelf Life:** By eliminating moisture, the freeze-drying method stops the growth of mold and germs. Because of this, freeze-dried candy has a longer shelf life than regular sweets, which makes it a reliable and practical snack choice.

4. **Retained Nutritional Value:** The candy's vitamins and minerals are preserved thanks to the process of freeze-drying. For individuals who prefer a sweet treat with some nutritional value, this can be especially advantageous.

5. **No Artificial Preservatives**: The candy's shelf life is naturally extended by the freeze-drying process, so extra artificial preservatives are rarely necessary. Customers who want natural and less processed snacks may find this attractive.

6. **Perfect for Grab-and-Go Snacking:** Candy that has been freeze-dried is a useful option for on-the-go snacking because it is lightweight. Because it is lightweight and portable, it can be used for outdoor pursuits like hiking, camping, or as a carry-along sweet treat.

7. **Unique Texture and Appearance**: The candy's porous and freeze-popped structure is produced by the process of freeze-drying. Customers may

find freeze-dried candy visually appealing and fascinating due to its distinct texture and look.

8. **Flexibility in Uses for Culinary**: Candy that has been freeze-dried can be crumbled or crushed and added as a garnish to yogurt, cereal, or desserts. Because of its many culinary uses, it can be a creative addition to a variety of cuisines.

9. **Fun and Novelty element**: Freeze-dried candy's distinct look, rich flavor, and crunchy texture all add to its overall fun and novelty element. It's a fun choice for people who want to explore new flavors in the confectionery industry.

WHAT DOES FREEZE-DRIED CANDY TASTE LIKE?

The flavor, color components, and scents of candy whether sour or sweet are all retained when it is freeze-dried, but the texture is entirely changed. Because there is no liquid left in the candy, most freeze-dried candies have an incredible crunch.

ARE FREEZE-DRIED CANDY HEALTHIER?

Candy that has been freeze-dried often has less moisture and the same quantity of nutrients as conventional candy. Candies that have been freeze-dried for up to 25 years are better for your teeth, especially if you wear braces! You can eat it all without worrying about breaking a tooth if you find it six months after Halloween because it doesn't go hard like ordinary candy does.

ARE THE CALORIES OF FREEZE-DRIED CANDY HIGHER?

Candy that has been freeze-dried contains no more calories than ordinary candy. Although freeze-drying produces amazing textures, it just removes moisture from candy; as a result, the calorie content remains the same as with traditional candy.

ARE YOU ABLE TO EAT FREEZE-DRIED CANDY?

Like with all candy and sweets, because it's largely sugar, freeze-dried candy should be consumed as part of a well-balanced diet. When enjoying your taste adventure with freeze-dried candy, remember to stay hydrated as it has the same amount of nutrients as conventional candy but with less moisture!

WHAT IS THE TIME NEEDED TO FREEZE-DRY CANDY?

The machine you use and the candy's moisture content will determine this. While some can be available in as short as 5–6 hours, others can take up to 24!

IS IT POSSIBLE TO USE DRY ICE TO FREEZE CANDY?

Yes you can freeze-dry candy with dry ice at home. However, we advise buying professionally freeze-dried sweets if you want to easily and securely enjoy the entire favorite experience. It's a taste adventure, we assure you! Let's enjoy ourselves!

FREEZE CANDY GIST

ooooooooooooooooooooooooooooooooooooo

Candy that has been freeze-dried has an incredible intensified taste. Fun aspects of the candy include its texture and how some of it swells. Like caramels, certain candy swell up to several times their initial size. Since freeze-dried candy is a treat during stressful times, it's a wise idea to include it in your emergency food collection.

You've undoubtedly noticed that freeze-dried candy isn't inexpensive if you've seen it in stores. For a very reasonable price, freeze-dried candies are a wonderful gift for your neighbors or coworkers if you have a freeze dryer at home. People are eager to try them since they are a delightful novelty.

All it takes to make freeze-dried candies into a present is to place them in adorable sealed jars or cellophane gift bags. You can get them a sampler pack or jar with a single type of freeze-dried candy, or you can choose a variety pack.

Best-Loved Freeze-Dried Candies

The greatest candies are those with some moisture content (not from oil). Certain candy, such as jelly beans, don't really change. Successful candies will have a crisp texture.

My preferred candies are:

★ **Skittles**: The strong flavor is addictive, and the crisp texture is ideal. I think the most well-liked freeze-dried candy is Skittles.

★ **Bit-O-Honey** still tastes amazing, but now you can savor it with this extra texture.

★ Caramel: Freeze-dried, these are really sweet and do not cling to your teeth.

★ **Riesen**: We call these enormous cocoa puffs. To satisfy your craving for chocolate, you should freeze-dry Riesen since chocolate that is high in fat doesn't last well.

Others suggested (though we haven't yet tried):

- Chews from Charleston
- Milky Duds
- Junior mints
- Now and Later
- Laffy Taffy
- Nerds
- Candy Bears
- Salt water taffy
- Cotton Candy
- Jolly ranchers

Which Candy Isn't Good at Freezing Drying?
- High-fat confections, like: chocolate, such as truffles or M&Ms
- Candy bars
- Candies with peanut butter inside, such as Reese's Pieces

Note: They will freeze dry if there is a thin layer of chocolate on the outside, similar to Riesen.

Candy with a low moisture content:
- Jelly beans
- Gumdrops
- Drops of lemon

Concise Overview of Freeze-Dry Candy Method

oooooooooooooooooooooooooooooooooooooooooo

Make Your Own Freeze-Dried Candies in a Freeze Dryer

It is assumed that you own a freeze-drying machine for these instructions. A freeze-drying machine, in my opinion, works best for freezing dry materials.

Procedures:
- ➢ Get the right amount and variety of candies.
- ➢ Get your chilling process freeze-dried started.
- ➢ Line the freeze-dryer pans with silicone mats or parchment paper.
- ➢ For optimal results, make sure the candy is in little pieces.
- ➢ Arrange candies on plates in a single layer. To give the candy room to expand, it is a good idea to space them apart. Jolly Ranchers, Reisen, caramel, and Milk Duds are among the candies that will swell to nearly three times their initial size. Reminder: Skittles don't need to be spaced apart. When they enlarge, they will move.
- ➢ To make it simple to identify the matching candy once they are freeze-dried, I lay the wrapper next

14

to the appropriate candy when I arrange the candies on my freeze-dryer trays.

➢ Make sure the candies are positioned correctly when you carefully place the trays in the vacuum chamber of your freeze-dryer.

➢ To finish the freeze-drying process and eliminate the water content, adhere to the manufacturer's instructions.

➢ As soon as the freeze-drying process is finished, place the candies in the appropriate storage. (See the section below for storage requirements.) As soon as freeze-dried candies are not stored in an airtight container, they will start to collect moisture from the surrounding air. The drying period with the freeze dryer is approximately 6-32 hours (see note below).

Freeze-Dry Candy and Get Result With Dry Ice

Candies with a specific texture can be made in a novel and enjoyable way by freeze-drying them with dry ice. This will assist you in creating the Best DIY freeze-dried candy with dry ice:

Material Needed:
★ **Supplies Required Candy:** High-sugar candies are the ones that freeze-dry better. Candy with fruit flavors, marshmallows, gummy bears, and even chocolate-covered candy are a few examples.

★ **Dry Ice:** Get dry ice from a nearby vendor. Wearing gloves with insulation, handle it carefully.

★ **Insulated Cooler:** To keep the candies and dry ice contained, use an insulated cooler. Make sure it has a tight-sealing cover.

★ **Silpat or Parchment Paper:** To stop sweets from sticking, line the cooler with silicone baking mats or parchment paper.

★ **Mesh Strainer:** Helps to separate candies from the dry ice easily.

★ **Mallet or hammer:** To break up the dry ice into tiny pieces.

★ **Storage:** The freeze-dried sweets should be kept in food-grade sealable bags or airtight containers.

Method:

1. Get the Candies Ready: Select the candies that you wish to freeze-dry. Candy with fillings that might not freeze dry well should be avoided.

After sorting them, discard any unnecessary wrappers.

2. Crush the Dry Ice: Using a mallet or hammer, carefully crush the dry ice into small, pea-sized bits. Ensure appropriate ventilation and utilize gloves to protect your hands.

3. Layering in the Cooler: Use parchment paper or a Silpat mat to line the bottom of the insulated cooler.

Cover the bottom with a layer of crushed dry ice.

4. Candy Placement: Place the candies over the sheet of dry ice. And ensure they are not touching each other.

5. Dry Ice Layers: Cover the candies with an additional layer of crushed dry ice.

Until the cooler is filled, keep adding layers of dry ice and candies alternately. Add a layer of dry ice on top to finish.

6. Sealing the Cooler: Tightly close the cooler and, if necessary, use tape to fill any gaps. Reducing air exchange is the main objective.

7. Await Freeze-Drying: Give the candies a minimum of 12 to 24 hours to freeze-dry. More moisture will be eliminated the longer you wait.

8. Examine and Adjust: Continually examine the candy to ensure the appropriate level of dryness. Adapt the time as necessary.

9. Remove and Store: After the candies have freeze-dried, take them out of the dry ice by straining them through a mesh strainer.
Keep the candies in food-grade sealable bags or airtight containers.

<u>**Advice:**</u>
- **Try a Variety of Candies:** See which ones freeze-dry the best and satisfy your palate.
- **Texture Control:** To achieve a range of textures from slightly chewy to completely crunchy, modify the freeze-drying duration.
- **Prevent Moisture:** To stop candies from absorbing moisture, keep the process in a dry atmosphere.
- When handling dry ice, don't forget to take safety precautions including wearing gloves and making sure there is enough air. Savor the homemade candies that you freeze-dried!

Note: Skittles should only be added at the very end for drying purposes because they do not require to go through the full freeze-drying procedure. That's where you'll save many hours of work.

30+ Holistic Recipes Including DIY Freeze-Dry Mastery Guide For Each

ooooooooooooooooooooooooooooooooooooooo

1. Colorful Skittles

<u>Ingredients</u>
- 1 cup of sugar, granulated
- two tsp water
- Half a teaspoon of flavoring essence (strawberry, orange, lemon, etc.)
- Food coloring in a range of hues
- Powdered sugar or cornstarch (for coating)

<u>Method:</u>
- ➢ Get the sugar syrup ready.
- ➢ Place water and granulated sugar in a saucepan and heat over medium heat.
- ➢ Until the sugar is entirely dissolved, stir continually.
- ➢ Once the mixture reaches a boil, reduce heat, and simmer until the mixture reaches the soft crack stage, which is around 270°F/132°C, a few minutes.
- ➢ Taste and Color of the Syrup: Take the syrup off the burner and let it to cool a little.
- ➢ Add your preferred flavoring extract and stir.

➢ To generate multiple hues, divide the syrup into smaller dishes and add different food coloring to each bowl.

➢ Shape the Skittles: Place little amounts of the colored syrup onto a silicone mold or a parchment paper-lined surface using a small dropper or syringe.

➢ Permit the droplets to solidify and cool. To expedite the procedure, you can put the mold in the refrigerator.

➢ Coat with Powder: After the droplets have solidified, gently coat them with powdered sugar or cornstarch by tossing them in a bowl. This keeps them from adhering to one another.

➢ Let Them Dry: To get rid of extra powder, let the Skittles dry entirely.

➢ After they have dried, store your homemade Skittles in an airtight container before enjoying them. They're prepared for enjoyment!

➢ Remember that this is a simplified recipe; more sophisticated equipment and procedures are used in the commercial production of Skittles. It can also be difficult to replicate the precise flavor and texture of store-bought Skittles at home, but this recipe offers an enjoyable method to make your own vibrant, bite-sized candy.

How to Freeze-Dryer Skittles:

Components and Tools:

- **Select Your Skittles:** Select a range of Skittles flavors to freeze-dry. You can have a variety of tastes in your freeze-dried Skittles, or concentrate on just one.
- **Invest in a Freeze Dryer:** Invest in or rent a user-friendly freeze-drying machine for your house.
- **Sort Skittles:** If you want to freeze-dry particular combinations of Skittles, sort them by to color or flavor.
- **Put the Required Tools Together:** Assemble trays or other storage units to hold the Skittles as they freeze-dry.

The Freeze-Drying Method:

1. Load the freeze-dryer
2. Ensure that the sorted Skittles are uniformly spaced out on the freeze drier trays.

Establish Freeze Dryer Settings:

3. For detailed instructions, refer to the freeze dryer's handbook. Usually, lower the temperature and modify the vacuum pressure in accordance with the machine's instructions.

Begin the cycle of freeze-drying:

4. Initiate the freeze-drying process. The machine will remove moisture from the Skittles by progressively lowering the temperature.

5. Consistently assess the Skittles' advancement as part of the process monitoring. The time frame might be different, although it might take a day or two. Make sure that the Skittles are crispy and completely dried.

After Freeze Drying:
- Verify Dryness Make sure the Skittles are completely dry so they have a light and crispy texture.
- Cool Down: Before handling, let the freeze-dried Skittles come to room temperature.

How to Store Them: To keep the freeze-dried Skittles crisp, store them in airtight jars or vacuum-sealed bags.

Remarks and Advice:
- ★ **Try Smaller Batches:** To get a better understanding of the unique characteristics of your freeze dryer, try smaller batches on your initial try.
- ★ **Record Your Method:** Record the length of time, the temperature, and any modifications you make while the process is freeze-drying. This documentation will assist you in improving your method for upcoming runs.
- ★ **Have patience:** Depending on the candy and the machine, freeze-drying can take several hours or even days. To get the intended outcomes, patience is essential.

★ Based on your observations made throughout the operation and the particular features of your freeze dryer, modify the duration.

2. Licorice Bites:

Ingredients
- one cup of flour
- half a cup of sugar
- 1/4 cup of butter without salt
- One-fourth cup molasses
- One tsp of anise essence
- One-half tsp baking soda
- 1/4 tsp salt

Coating: Dusting with powdered sugar

Tools:
- bowl for mixing
- Saute pan
- Paper parchment
- rolling pin
- Slicer or paring knife
- The freezer dryer
- Vacuum pump (should the freeze dryer not have one built in)
- Freeze dryer trays
- airtight bag or vacuum-sealed container

Making Licorice Bites:
➢ To prepare the dough, put the flour, sugar, molasses, unsalted butter, baking soda, salt, and anise extract in a mixing bowl. Blend until a uniform dough is formed.

➢ **Roll Out Dough:** Using a surface dusted with flour, roll out the licorice dough into a thin, uniform rectangle.

➢ **Cut into Strips:** To create licorice-like forms, cut the rolled-out dough into thin strips using a knife or pizza cutter.

➢ **Let Set:** To make the licorice bites a little harder, let them sit for a few minutes.

➢ **Dust with Powdered Sugar:** To keep the licorice bits from sticking, dust them with powdered sugar.

➢ **Organize on trays:** Arrange the licorice bites so that they are evenly dried on freeze-dryer trays.

The Freeze-Drying Method:

★ **Setting Up for Freeze Drying:** Before freeze-drying, let the licorice bites sit for a few minutes.

★ **How to Fill the Freeze Dryer:** In accordance with the manufacturer's recommendations, preheat the freeze dryer.

★ **Place Bites on Trays:** Using freeze-dryer trays, place the licorice bites, being sure to arrange them properly.

★ **Establish Freeze Dryer Settings:** Aim for a low temperature of approximately -20°F to -40°F (-29°C to -40°C) for the freeze dryer, and follow the machine's instructions for adjusting the vacuum pressure.

★ **Start the Cycle of Freeze-Drying:** Begin the process of freeze-drying. The device will start to gently reduce the temperature and remove the moisture from the bites of licorice.

★ **Keep an eye on the process:** Make sure to periodically monitor the freeze-drying cycle's progress. The time frame might be different, although it might take a day or two. As necessary, adjust the settings.

★ **Verify the Dryness:** Make sure the licorice bites that have been freeze-dried are completely dry. Their texture need to be crisp and airy.

★ **Cool Down:** Before handling, let the freeze-dried licorice bites come to room temperature.

★ **Keep Safe:** To preserve their crispness, store the freeze-dried licorice bites in an airtight receptacle or vacuum-sealed bag.

Advice and Adaptations:

- **Try Different Extract tastes:** To make the licorice bites unique, experiment with tastes like vanilla or raspberry.

- **Add Food Coloring (optional):** To create a colorful variety of licorice bites, divide the dough and add food coloring.

- **Roll in Extra Sugar (Optional):** For a sweeter coating, roll the licorice bits in extra sugar.

- **Form into Twists (Recommended):** For a traditional licorice twist, twist together pairs of strips before freezing-drying them.

- **Present Packaging:** For a charming handcrafted present, place the freeze-dried licorice nibbles inside attractive bags or boxes.

3. Chocolate Almond Clusters

Ingredients

- Two cups of whole or sliced almonds
- One cup of chocolate chips, either milk, white, or dark chocolate
- Two tsp of coconut oil
- 1/4 cup powdered sugar; dusting is optional.

Tools:

- bowl for mixing
- Safe-for-microwave bowl or dual boiler
- utensil or spatula
- Paper parchment
- baking sheet
- The freezer dryer
- Vacuum pump (should the freeze dryer not have one built in)
- Freeze dryer trays
- Airtight bag or vacuum-sealed container

How to Make Chocolate Almond Clusters:

- ➢ **Chocolate Melt:** Melt the chocolate chips and coconut oil in a bowl that is safe to use in the microwave or over a double boiler, stirring until smooth.
- ➢ **Mix with Almonds:** Pour the melted chocolate over the almonds and toss until they are evenly covered.
- ➢ Drop Spoonfuls of the chocolate-almond mixture onto a baking sheet coated with parchment paper, making clusters, using a spoon or spatula.

- ➤ **Dust with Powdered Sugar (Optional):** For an additional sweetness boost, feel free to dust the clusters with powdered sugar.
- ➤ **Allow to Set:** Until the chocolate solidifies, let the chocolate almond clusters sit at room temperature or chill in the refrigerator.
- ➤ After the clusters have set, place them on freeze-dryer trays, making sure to position them evenly so that the freeze-drying process can begin.

The Freeze-Drying Method:

- ★ **Setting Up for Freeze Desiccation**: Before freeze-drying, let the chocolate almond clusters cool fully.
- ★ **How to Fill the Freeze Dryer:** In accordance with the manufacturer's recommendations, preheat the freeze dryer.
- ★ **Arrange Groups on Trays:** Place the chocolate almond clusters on the trays of the freeze-dryer, making sure that they are well separated.
- ★ **Establish Freeze Dryer Settings:** Aim for a low temperature of approximately -20°F to -40°F (-29°C to -40°C) for the freeze dryer, and follow the machine's instructions for adjusting the vacuum pressure.
- ★ **Start the Cycle of Freeze-Drying:** Begin the process of freeze-drying. The chocolate almond clusters will begin to lose moisture as the machine progressively reduces the temperature.
- ★ **Keep an eye on the process:** Make sure to periodically monitor the freeze-drying cycle's

progress. The time frame might be different, although it might take a day or two. As necessary, adjust the settings.

★ **Verify the Dryness:** Ensure that the freeze-dried chocolate almond clusters are thoroughly dry. Their texture need to be crisp and airy.

★ **Cool Down:** Before handling, let the chocolate almond clusters that have been freeze-dried come to room temperature.

★ **Keep Safe:** To preserve their crispness, store the freeze-dried chocolate almond clusters in an airtight receptacle or vacuum-sealed bag.

Advice and Adaptations:

- **Add some dried fruit (Optional):** For extra sweetness, stir in some dried fruit pieces, like raisins or cranberries, to the chocolate-almond mixture.

- **Drizzle with White Chocolate (Optional):** To add a decorative touch, pour melted white chocolate over the clusters after they have freeze-dried.

- **Sprinkle the clusters with sea salt (Optional):** To create a contrast between the flavors of sweetness and salt.

- **Form Bite-Sized Groups:** For a treat that is bite-sized, create smaller clusters.

- **Present Boxes:** For a charming homemade gift, package the freeze-dried chocolate almond clusters in attractive bags or boxes.

4. Cherry Almond Bars
Composition:
Regarding the Base:
- One cup of almond flour
- Half a cup of melted unsalted butter
- 1/4 cup of sugar, granulated
- One tsp almond extract

For the filling:
- Salt pinch
- One cup of chopped dried cherries
- half a cup of cherry preserves
- One-fourth cup almond flour

Regarding the Topping:
- Half a cup of almonds, sliced
- 1/4 cup powdered sugar; dusting is optional.
- Tools:
- 9x9-inch baking dish for mixing
- Paper parchment
- The freezer dryer
- Vacuum pump (should the freeze dryer not have one built in)
- Freeze dryer trays
- Airtight bag or vacuum-sealed container

Almond Cherry Bars Getting ready:
- ➤ **Set Up the Base:** Almond flour, melted butter, granulated sugar, almond essence, and a small amount of salt should all be combined in a mixing dish. Blend until thoroughly blended.
- ➤ **Press into Baking Dish:** To create an even base, press the almond flour mixture firmly into

the bottom of a 9 by 9-inch baking dish lined with parchment paper.

➢ To make the filling, combine the almond flour, cherry preserves, and chopped dried cherries in a separate bowl. Evenly distribute this mixture over the base of almond flour.

➢ **Almond Slices:** Evenly distribute the almond slices over the cherry filling, gently pushing them into the mixture.

➢ **Permit to Set:** Put the cherry almond bars in the fridge to firm up, preferably for two to three hours.

Utilizing Freeze-Drying Method:

Getting Ready for Freeze Drying Before freeze-drying, let the cherry almond bars cool fully.

★ **How to Fill the Freeze Dryer:** In accordance with the manufacturer's recommendations, preheat the freeze dryer.

★ **Slice into Bars:** Using a sharp knife, cut the package of cherry almond bars into separate bars or squares.

★ **Set Bars Aside on Trays:** Make sure the cut bars are uniformly spaced when you arrange them the freeze dryer trays.

★ **Establish Freeze Dryer Settings:** Aim for a low temperature of approximately -20°F to -40°F (-29°C to -40°C) for the freeze dryer, and follow the machine's instructions for adjusting the vacuum pressure.

★ **Start the Freeze-Drying Cycle:** The freeze-drying procedure should be started. The device will start the process of removing moisture from the cherry almond bars by progressively lowering the temperature.

★ **Keep an eye on the process:** Make sure to periodically monitor the freeze-drying cycle's progress. The time frame might be different, although it might take a day or two. As necessary, adjust the settings.

★ **Verify the Dryness:** Make sure the cherry almond bars that have been freeze-dried are completely dry. Their texture need to be crisp and airy.

★ **Cool Down:** Before handling, let the cherry almond bars that have been freeze-dried come to room temperature.

★ If desired, add a little extra sweetness to the freeze-dried cherry almond bars by dusting them with powdered sugar.

★ **Keep Safe:** To preserve their crispness, store the freeze-dried cherry almond bars in an airtight jar or vacuum-sealed bag.

Advice and Adaptations:

- **Try It with Different Fruits:** For variation, try using dried cranberries or apricots instead of dried cherries.

- **Drizzle White Chocolate (Optional):** For a finishing touch, pour melted white chocolate over the cherry almond bars once they have freeze-dried.

- **Incorporate Lemon or Orange Zest (Optional):** into the Cherry Filling to Give It a Hint of Citrus Flavor.
- **Serve Whipped Cream (Optional):** For a wonderful treat, serve freeze-dried cherry almond bars with a scoop of whipped cream.
- **Present Boxes:** For charming homemade gift, package the freeze-dried cherry almond bars in attractive bags or boxes.

5. Yogurt and Fruit Bites

Components:

Regarding the Yogurt and Fruit Mixture:
- 1 cup of mixed berries, including raspberries, blueberries, and strawberries
- One cup of Greek yogurt
- Two tablespoons of maple syrup or honey
- One tsp vanilla essence

Regarding the Topping:
- Granola (Optional)
- Extra berries (Optional)

Tools:
- Food processor or blender
- Paper parchment
- Freezer or dehydrator
- Vacuum pump (should the freeze dryer not have one built in)
- Freeze-dryer or dehydrator trays
- Airtight bag or vacuum-sealed container

How to Make Fruit and Yogurt Bites:

- ➢ **Assemble the yogurt and fruit mixture**: In a blender or food processor, combine mixed berries, Greek yogurt, honey or maple syrup, and vanilla extract. Process till smooth.
- ➢ **Spread on Parchment:** Spread parchment paper on a baking sheet or tray. To make a thin layer, evenly distribute the fruit and yogurt mixture onto the parchment paper.
- ➢ **Optional Toppings:** For more texture and taste, top the fruit and yogurt mixture with extra berries and granola if you'd like.
- ➢ **Freeze or Dehydrate:** Follow the manufacturer's instructions to dehydrate the mixture in a dehydrator, or freeze it for a few hours until it solidifies.

The Freeze-Drying Method:

- ★ **Setting Up for Freeze Drying:** Before moving on to the freeze-drying stage, let the mixture thaw a little if you decide to freeze it.
- ★ **Cut into Bite-Sized Pieces:** Using a knife or cookie cutters, cut the fruit and yogurt mixture into bite-sized pieces when it has solidified.
- ★ **How to Fill the Freeze Dryer:** In accordance with the manufacturer's recommendations, preheat the freeze dryer.
- ★ **Spoon Bits onto Trays:** Place the chopped fruit and yogurt bits in an equal layer on freeze-dryer trays.
- ★ **Configure Freeze Dryer Parameters:** Follow the machine's instructions to modify the vacuum

pressure and set the temperature to a low range of -20°F to -40°F (-29°C to -40°C).

★ **Start the Cycle of Freeze-Drying:** Begin the process of freeze-drying. The device will start to gently reduce the temperature and remove moisture from the yogurt and fruit bits.

★ **Keep an eye on the process:** Make sure to periodically monitor the freeze-drying cycle's progress. The time frame might be different, although it might take a day or two. As necessary, adjust the settings.

★ **Verify the Dryness:** Make sure the yogurt bites and freeze-dried fruit are completely dry. Their texture need to be crisp and airy.

★ **Cool Down:** Before handling, let the yogurt bites and freeze-dried fruit come to room temperature.

★ **Keep Safe:** To keep the fruit and yogurt bites crisp, store them in an airtight receptacle or vacuum-sealed bag.

Advice and Adaptations:

• **Try Different Fruit Combinations:** Experiment with different fruit combinations to get a range of flavors.

• **Add chopped nuts or seeds (Optional):** You can it to the fruit and yogurt mixture to give it a crunchier texture.

• **Drizzle with Honey (Optional):** For an added sweetness, drizzle honey over the bite-sized freeze-dried treats.

- **Serve as Frozen Treats:** For a cool frozen treat, eat the fruit and yogurt pieces straight out of the freezer.
- **Present Boxes:** For a charming homemade gift, present the freeze-dried fruit and yogurt nibbles in attractive bags or boxes.

6. Gummy Mango Chili Lollipops
Components:
For the base of mango chili:
- Two ripe mangos, chopped and peeled
- 1/2 cup of sugar, granulated
- One tablespoon of lime juice
- 1 tsp chile powder, or more according to taste
- A dash of salt

For the Molds of Lollipops:
- Lollipop sticks
- Molds for lollipops

Tools:
- food processor or blender
- Saute pan
- Molds for lollipops
- Popsicles
- Freezer or dehydrator
- Vacuum pump (should the freeze dryer not have one built in)
- Freeze-dryer or dehydrator trays
- Airtight bag or vacuum-sealed container

Making Mango Chili Lollipops:

➢ **Get the Mango Chili Base ready:** Diced mangos, granulated sugar, lime juice, chili powder, and a little amount of salt should all be combined into a smooth puree in a food processor or blender.

➢ **Simmer Mango Mixture:** Pour the pureed mango into a saucepan and simmer, stirring often, over medium heat until it thickens. Let the simmer mango mixture cool down a little bit.

➢ **Fill Molds for lollipops**: Fill lollipop molds with the mango-chile mixture, making sure to leave a tiny opening at the top for the lollipop sticks.

➢ **Put the lollipops in**: Make sure the lollipop sticks are centered in each lollipop by inserting them into the molds.

➢ **Freeze or Dehydrate:** You may either follow the manufacturer's instructions and dehydrate the lollipops in a dehydrator, or you can freeze them for a few hours until solid.

The Freeze-Drying Method:

★ **Setting Up for Freeze Drying:** Before moving on to the freeze-drying stage, let the lollipops thaw a little if you decide to freeze them.

★ **How to Fill the Freeze Dryer:** In accordance with the manufacturer's recommendations, preheat the freeze dryer.

★ **Place Candy on Trays:** Place the lollipops on the freeze-dryer trays, making sure they are not in contact with one another and equally spaced.

★ **Establish Freeze Dryer Settings:** Aim for a low temperature of approximately -20°F to -40°F (-29°C to -40°C) for the freeze dryer, and follow the machine's instructions for adjusting the vacuum pressure.

★ **Start the Cycle of Freeze-Drying:** Begin the process of freeze-drying. The mango chili lollipops will begin to lose moisture as the machine progressively lowers the temperature.

★ **Keep an eye on the process:** Make sure to periodically monitor the freeze-drying cycle's progress. The time frame might be different, although it might take a day or two. As necessary, adjust the settings.

★ **Verify the Dryness:** Make sure the mango chili lollipops are completely dry after freeze-drying them. Their texture need to be crisp and airy.

★ **Cool Down:** Before handling, let the mango chili lollipops that have been freeze-dried come to room temperature.

★ **Keep Safe:** To keep the mango chili lollipops crisp, store them in an airtight container or vacuum-sealed bag.

Advice and Adaptations:

- **Adjust Chili Powder (Optional):** To customize the lollipops' level of spiciness, add or subtract chili powder according to your preference.

- **Add Tajin or Season Salt (Optional):** Garnish the lollipops with seasoned salt or Tajin to add an additional taste layer.

- **Try Different Fruit Combinations:** For a distinctive taste, try combining mango with other tropical fruits like passion fruit or pineapple.
- **Serve with Chamoy Dip:** Make a chamoy dip to go with mango chili lollipops for a classic Mexican flavor combination.
- **Gift Packaging:** For a charming handmade present, encase the freeze-dried mango chili lollipops in attractive bags or boxes.

7. The Best Handmade Riesen
Components:
- One cup of caramel chews or candies
- One cup of chocolate chips, either milk or dark chocolate
- One tablespoon of butter without salt
- 1/2 cup of optionally chopped pecans or almonds
- Sea salt (optional) for sprinkling

Tools:
- Saucepan
- Microwave-safe bowl
- Paper parchment
- Baking dish
- The freezer dryer
- Vacuum pump (should the freeze dryer not have one built in)
- Freeze dryer trays
- Airtight bag or vacuum-sealed container

- **Get the baking dish ready:** Using parchment paper, line a baking dish, providing an overhang for simple removal.
- **Melt Caramels:** Melt the caramel candies in a saucepan over low heat, stirring all the time. As an alternative, microwave them in short bursts in a bowl that is safe for the microwave.
- **Optional Nut Addition:** Feel free to incorporate finely chopped nuts or almonds into the melting caramel.
- **In a baking dish, spread:** Evenly distribute the melted caramel mixture throughout the baking dish after pouring it in.
- **Cool and set:** Let the caramel cool and set in the fridge for a minimum of one to two hours, or until it becomes solid.
- **Cut into Pieces:** After the caramel sets completely, remove it from the baking dish by using the overhanging parchment paper. Chop it up into small pieces.
- **Melt Chocolate:** In a basin that is safe to use in the microwave, quickly melt the chocolate chips and unsalted butter together, stirring in between each burst until the mixture is smooth.
- **Dip Caramel Pieces:** Make sure every piece of caramel is completely covered by dipping it into the melted chocolate. Reposition the coated parts onto the parchment paper.
- **Sprinkle Sea Salt (Optional):** To create a contrast between sweetness and saltiness, you

can optionally sprinkle some sea salt on top of the caramel pieces covered in chocolate.

> **Allow to Set:** Place the caramel pieces covered in chocolate in the refrigerator and let them sit there for approximately an hour, or until the chocolate solidifies.

The Freeze-Drying Method:

★ **Getting Ready for Freeze-Drying:** Before freeze-drying, let the caramel pieces coated in chocolate cool fully.

★ **How to Fill the Freeze Dryer:** In accordance with the manufacturer's recommendations, preheat the freeze dryer.

★ **Arrange Parts on Trays:** Place the caramel pieces coated in chocolate on freeze-dryer trays, being sure to space them properly.

★ **Configure Freeze Dryer Parameters:** Follow the machine's instructions to modify the vacuum pressure and set the temperature to a low range of -20°F to -40°F (-29°C to -40°C).

★ **Start the Cycle of Freeze-Drying:** Begin the process of freeze-drying. The chocolate-coated caramel chunks will begin to lose moisture as the machine gradually reduces the temperature.

★ **Keep an eye on the process:** Make sure to periodically monitor the freeze-drying cycle's progress. The time frame might be different, although it might take a day or two. As necessary, adjust the settings.

- ★ **Verify the Dryness:** Make sure the Riesen pieces are completely dry after freeze-drying them. Their texture need to be crisp and airy.
- ★ **Cool Down:** Before handling, let the freeze-dried Riesen pieces come to room temperature.
- ★ **Keep Safe:** To preserve their crispness, store the freeze-dried Riesen pieces in an airtight container or vacuum-sealed bag.

Advice and Adaptations:
- **Experiment with Nuts:** Try a variety of nuts or a blend of them to get a range of flavors and textures.
- **Drizzle with White Chocolate (Optional):** For a decorative touch, pour melted white chocolate over the freeze-dried Riesen pieces.
- **Add Espresso Powder (Optional):** To add a hint of coffee flavor to the melted chocolate, stir in a little pinch of espresso powder.
- **Cut into Bite-Sized Pieces:** To make a bite-sized treat, cut smaller Riesen pieces.
- **Present Boxes:** Pack the freeze-dried Riesen pieces in attractive bags or boxes for a beautiful homemade present.

8. My decadent Honey Bit-O
Components:
- One cup of honey
- One cup almond butter
- one cup sugar
- One tsp vanilla essence
- Half a teaspoon of extract from almonds
- A dash of salt
- one cup of almonds, chopped
- Parchment paper

Equipment:
- Saute pan
- A candy thermometer
- bowl for mixing
- Baking dish
- The freezer dryer
- Vacuum pump (should the freeze dryer not have one built in)
- Freeze dryer trays
- Airtight bag or vacuum-sealed container

Bit- O-Honey Getting ready:
- ➤ **Get the baking dish ready:** Using parchment paper, line a baking dish, providing an overhang for simple removal.
- ➤ **Prepare the honey mixture:** Put the almond butter, honey, sugar, vanilla, almond extract, and a small amount of salt in a saucepan. Stir until the sugar melts over a medium heat source.

➤ **Apply the Candy Thermometer:** Put a candy thermometer on top of the saucepan and cook the mixture until it reaches the hard-crack stage, which is around 300°F/149°C, while stirring all the time.

➤ **Include Sliced Almonds:** Add the chopped almonds and stir until they are well mixed into the mixture.

➤ **Transfer to Baking Dish:** Evenly distribute the heated honey and almond mixture into the baking dish that has been prepared.

➤ **Allow to chill:** Put the mixture in the refrigerator to chill and set for at least two to three hours, or until it is completely solid.

➤ **Sliced into Segments:** When the Bit-O-Honey is completely set, remove it from the baking dish by using the overhanging parchment paper. Chop it up into small pieces.

The Freeze-Drying Method:

★ **Setting Up for Freeze Drying:** Before freeze-drying, let the Bit-O-Honey bits cool fully.

★ **How to Fill the Freeze Dryer:** In accordance with the manufacturer's recommendations, preheat the freeze dryer.

★ **Arrange Parts on Trays:** Place the Bit-O-Honey bits in an equal layer on the freeze-dryer trays.

★ **Establish Freeze Dryer Settings:** Aim for a low temperature of approximately -20°F to -40°F (-29°C to -40°C) for the freeze dryer, and follow

the machine's instructions for adjusting the vacuum pressure.

★ **Start the Cycle of Freeze-Drying:** Begin the process of freeze-drying. The Bit-O-Honey chunks' moisture will be removed by the machine as it gradually lowers the temperature.

★ **Keep an eye on the process:** Make sure to periodically monitor the freeze-drying cycle's progress. The time frame might be different, although it might take a day or two. As necessary, adjust the settings.

★ **Verify the Dryness:** Make sure the Bit-O-Honey pieces have dried completely after being freeze-dried. Their texture need to be crisp and airy.

★ **Cool Down:** Before handling, let the freeze-dried Bit-O-Honey bits come to room temperature.

★ **Keep Safe:** To preserve their crispness, store the freeze-dried Bit-O-Honey bits in an airtight receptacle or vacuum-sealed bag.

Advice and Adaptations:

- **Chocolate Dipped (Optional):** Dip the freeze-dried Bit-O-Honey chunks in melted chocolate for an extra layer of taste.
- **Add the coconut flakes (Optional):** For a tropical flavor, top the chocolate covering with coconut flakes.
- **Mix with Other Nuts:** To create a variety of textures, try experimenting with various nuts or a combination of nuts.

44

- **Make a Variety of Flavors:** Divide the honey mixture and mix in various extracts to create a variety of Bit-O-Honey flavors.
- **Present Packaging:** For a charming handmade present, place the freeze-dried Bit-O-Honey pieces inside attractive bags or boxes.

9. Greatest DIY Milky Duds
Ingredients:
- 1 cup condensed milk with added sugar
- One cup of brown sugar
- half a cup of butter without salt
- one-fourth cup heavy cream
- One tsp vanilla essence
- A dash of salt
- 1 1/2 cups of chocolate chips (dark or milk chocolate) for the chocolate coating
- One tablespoon of coconut oil

Tools:
- Saute pan
- A candy thermometer
- Paper parchment
- Baking dish
- The freezer dryer
- Vacuum pump (should the freeze dryer not have one built in)
- Freeze dryer trays
- Airtight bag or vacuum-sealed container

Milky Duds Getting ready:

➢ **Get the baking dish ready:** Using parchment paper, line a baking dish, providing an overhang for simple removal.

➢ **Mix the ingredients together:** Brown sugar, unsalted butter, heavy cream, vanilla extract, sweetened condensed milk, and a small amount of salt should all be combined in a pot.

➢ **Warm Milk Dud Concoction:** Using a candy thermometer, stir the mixture over medium heat until it reaches the soft-ball stage, which is approximately 240°F or 116°C.

➢ **Transfer to Baking Dish:** Evenly distribute the heated milk dud mixture throughout the baking dish after pouring it in.

➢ **Allow to Cool:** Refrigerate the mixture for at least two to three hours, or until it is completely set.

➢ **Cut into Pieces:** After the Milk Duds are completely set, remove them from the baking dish by using the overhanging parchment paper. Chop them up into little pieces.

The Freeze-Drying Method:

★ **Getting Ready for Freeze Drying:** Before freeze-drying, let the Milk Duds pieces cool fully.

★ **How to Fill the Freeze Dryer:** In accordance with the manufacturer's recommendations, preheat the freeze dryer.

★ **Arrange Parts on Trays:** Place the Milk Duds pieces in an equal layer on the freeze-dryer trays.

★ **Establish Freeze Dryer Settings:** Aim for a low temperature of approximately -20°F to -40°F (-29°C to -40°C) for the freeze dryer, and follow the machine's instructions for adjusting the vacuum pressure.

★ **Start the Cycle of Freeze-Drying:** Begin the process of freeze-drying. The device will start to gently reduce the Milk Duds pieces' temperature and remove moisture from them.

★ **Keep an eye on the process:** Make sure to periodically monitor the freeze-drying cycle's progress. The time frame might be different, although it might take a day or two. As necessary, adjust the settings.

★ **Verify the Dryness:** Make sure the chunks of Milk Duds that have been freeze-dried are completely dry. Their texture need to be crisp and airy.

★ **Cool Down:** Before handling, let the freeze-dried Milk Duds pieces come to room temperature.

★ **Get the chocolate coating ready:** In a bowl that is safe to put in the microwave or with a double boiler, melt chocolate chips and coconut oil together.

★ **Dip Milk Duds in Chocolate:** Make sure every freeze-dried Milk Dud piece is completely covered by dipping it into the melted chocolate.

Back on the parchment paper, place the coated pieces.

★ **Allow to Set:** Place the Milk Duds covered in chocolate in the fridge and let them set for approximately an hour, or until the chocolate solidifies.

★ **Keep Safe:** Place the chocolate-coated, freeze-dried Milk Duds in an airtight container or vacuum-sealed bag to keep their crispiness.

Advice and Adaptations:

- **Add Sea Salt (Optional):** Garnish the chocolate coating with a small amount of sea salt to create a contrast between sweetness and saltiness.
- **Make a Variety of Coatings:** Try a variety of chocolate coatings, including dark or white chocolate, to add some variation.
- **Combine with Nuts (Optional):** To add extra crunch, stir chopped nuts into the Milk Dud mixture before adding it to the baking dish.
- **Gift Boxes:** For a charming homemade gift, present the freeze-dried and chocolate-coated Milk Duds in attractive boxes or bags.

10. Delectable Candies Bars

Components:

Base Components:

- Two cups chopped nuts (almonds, peanuts, or a combination),
- two bowls of rice cereal that is crunchy.
- One cup of maple syrup or honey

- One cup of nut butter (almond, cashew, or peanut butter)
- One tsp vanilla essence
- A dash of salt

The coating of chocolate:
- Two cups of chocolate chips, either milk, white, or dark.
- Two tsp of coconut oil

Equipment:
- Bowl for mixing
- Saute pan
- Paper parchment
- Baking dish
- The freezer dryer
- Vacuum pump (should the freeze dryer not have one built in)
- Freeze dryer trays
- Airtight bag or vacuum-sealed container

Candy Bars Getting ready:
- ➢ **Get the baking dish ready:** Using parchment paper, line a baking dish, providing an overhang for simple removal.
- ➢ **Mix the foundational ingredients:** Chopped nuts, crispy rice cereal, honey, maple syrup, nut butter, vanilla essence, and a dash of salt should all be combined in a mixing dish. Blend thoroughly until the components are dispersed equally.

- ➢ **Put into Baking Dish Press:** To ensure a uniform layer, press the mixture firmly into the baking dish that has been prepared.
- ➢ **Permit to Set:** Allow the base layer to firm completely, which should take at least two to three hours in the refrigerator.
- ➢ **Cut into Bars:** Using the overhanging parchment paper, carefully remove the base layer from the baking dish once it has solidified. Cut it into individual bars.

The Freeze-Drying Method:

- ★ **Setting Up for Freeze Desiccation:** Let the candy bars cool fully before freezing them.
- ★ **How to Fill the Freeze Dryer:** In accordance with the manufacturer's recommendations, preheat the freeze dryer.
- ★ **Set Bars Aside on Trays:** Place the candy bars in an equal layer on the freeze-dryer trays.
- ★ **Establish Freeze Dryer Settings:** Aim for a low temperature of approximately -20°F to -40°F (-29°C to -40°C) for the freeze dryer, and follow the machine's instructions for adjusting the vacuum pressure.
- ★ **Start the Cycle of Freeze-Drying:** Begin the process of freeze-drying. The device will start to gently reduce the candy bars' temperature and remove moisture from them.
- ★ **Keep an eye on the process:** Make sure to periodically monitor the freeze-drying cycle's progress. The time frame might be different,

although it might take a day or two. As necessary, adjust the settings.

★ **Verify the Dryness:** Make sure the candy bars that have been freeze-dried are completely dry. Their texture need to be crisp and airy.

★ **Cool Down:** Before handling, let the candy bars that have been freeze-dried come to room temperature.

★ Get the chocolate coating ready. In a bowl that is safe to put in the microwave or with a double boiler, melt chocolate chips and coconut oil together.

★ **Chocolate Dip Bars:** Make sure every freeze-dried candy bar is completely covered by dipping it into the melted chocolate. Back on the parchment paper, place the coated bars.

★ **Permit to Set:** Allow the candy bars covered in chocolate to set in the refrigerator for approximately one hour, or until the chocolate solidifies.

★ **Keep Safe:** To keep the chocolate-covered, freeze-dried candy bars crisp, store them in an airtight jar or vacuum-sealed bag.

Advice and Adaptations:

- **Try Out Some Nut Butters:** Use distinct nut butters, like cashew, peanut, or almond butter, to create interesting flavors.
- **Add Dried Fruit (Optional):** To increase the sweetness of the base mixture, stir in dried fruit pieces, such as raisins or cranberries.

- **Establish Layers:** To create a tiered look, sandwich layers of flavor-infused spreads or other nut butters between the chocolate covering and foundation.
- **Sprinkle Sea Salt (Optional):** For a contrast between sweet and salty, sprinkle some sea salt on top of the chocolate covering.
- **Present Boxes:** Present the freeze-dried, chocolate-coated candy bars in attractive boxes or bags to make a thoughtful homemade present.

11. Delicious Cinnamon Sugar Apple Slices
Ingredients:
- Six to eight medium-sized apples (ideally Honeycrisp or Gala, or another sweet kind)
- 1 cup of sugar, granulated
- two tsp finely ground cinnamon
- One-third cup lemon juice (to avoid browning)

Tools:
- Apple Slicer and Corer
- Bowl for mixing
- The freezer dryer
- Vacuum pump (should the freeze dryer not have one built in)
- Freeze dryer trays
- Airtight bag or vacuum-sealed container

How to Prepare Apple Slices with Cinnamon Sugar:

> **Get the apples ready:** Using an apple corer and slicer, wash, core, and cut the apples into uniform slices.

> **Stop Browning:** To keep the apple slices from browning, toss them in lemon juice. Ensure the slices are well-coated.

> **Apply Cinnamon Sugar Coat:** Ground cinnamon and granulated sugar should be combined in a mixing basin. After the apple slices are well coated, toss them in the cinnamon sugar mixture.

> **Arrange on Trays:** Evenly space out the covered apple slices on the trays of the freeze-dryer to ensure they dry completely.

The Freeze-Drying Method:

★ **Setting Up for Freeze Desiccation:** Before freeze-drying, let the apple slices coated in cinnamon sugar rest for a few minutes.

★ **How to Fill the Freeze Dryer:** In accordance with the manufacturer's recommendations, preheat the freeze dryer.

★ **Arrange Carafes of Slices:** Place the apple slices coated in cinnamon sugar on freeze-dryer trays, being sure to leave space between each one.

★ **Establish Freeze Dryer Settings:** Aim for a low temperature of approximately -20°F to -40°F (-29°C to -40°C) for the freeze dryer, and follow

the machine's instructions for adjusting the vacuum pressure.

★ **Start the Cycle of Freeze-Drying:** Begin the process of freeze-drying. The apple slices' moisture removal process will begin as the machine gradually reduces the temperature.

★ **Keep an eye on the process:** Make sure to periodically monitor the freeze-drying cycle's progress. The time frame might be different, although it might take a day or two. As necessary, adjust the settings.

★ **Verify the Dryness:** Make sure the cinnamon sugar apple slices that have been freeze-dried are completely dry. Their texture need to be crisp and airy.

★ **Cool Down:** Before handling, let the freeze-dried apple slices come to room temperature.

★ **Keep Safe:** To preserve their crispness, store the freeze-dried cinnamon sugar apple slices in an airtight receptacle or vacuum-sealed bag.

Advice and Adaptations:

- **Try Different Apple Varieties:** To experience a range of flavors and sensations, try several apple kinds.

- **Add Nutmeg or Allspice (Optional):** In order to improve the flavor profile, you can add a small pinch of either spice to the cinnamon sugar combination.

- **Serve with Dip (Optional):** To go with the freeze-dried apple slices, make a yogurt or caramel dip.
- **Produce Apple Chips:** For a texture akin to chips, finely slice the apples.
- **Present Packaging:** For a charming handcrafted present, arrange the freeze-dried cinnamon sugar apple slices in attractive bags or jars.

12. Homemade Coconut Macaroons: **Components:**
- Three cups of finely chopped coconut, either sweetened or not
- 1 cup condensed milk with added sugar
- One tsp vanilla essence
- Two big egg whites
- A dash of salt
- Melted chocolate or chocolate chips (optional, for dipping)

Tools:
- Bowl for mixing
- Whisk or electric mixer
- Baking sheet
- Paper parchment
- The freezer dryer
- Vacuum pump (should the freeze dryer not have one built in)
- Freeze dryer trays
- Airtight bag or vacuum-sealed container

Macaroons with coconuts Getting ready:

- ➢ **Warm up the oven:** Set the oven temperature to 325°F (163°C).
- ➢ **Combine Components:** Shredded coconut, sweetened condensed milk, vanilla essence, and a dash of salt should all be combined in a mixing dish. Blend thoroughly.
- ➢ **Whip Egg Whites:** Beat the egg whites in a another bowl until firm peaks form.
- ➢ **Fold in Egg Whites:** Using a gentle touch, thoroughly blend the whipped egg whites into the coconut mixture.
- ➢ **Form Macaroons:** To create macaroons, arrange small mounds of the coconut mixture on a baking sheet lined with parchment paper using a spoon or cookie scoop.
- ➢ **Bake:** Bake the macaroons for about 15 to 20 minutes, or until the edges are golden brown, in a preheated oven.
- ➢ **Cool:** On the baking sheet, let the coconut macaroons cool fully.

The Freeze-Drying Method:

- ★ **Setting Up for Freeze Drying:** Before freeze-drying, let the coconut macaroons come to room temperature.
- ★ **How to Fill the Freeze Dryer:** In accordance with the manufacturer's recommendations, preheat the freeze dryer.

★ **Place Macaroons on Trays:** Using a freeze-dryer tray, place the coconut macaroons, making sure to position them evenly.

★ **Establish Freeze Dryer Settings:** Aim for a low temperature of approximately -20°F to -40°F (-29°C to -40°C) for the freeze dryer, and follow the machine's instructions for adjusting the vacuum pressure.

★ **Start the Cycle of Freeze-Drying:** Begin the process of freeze-drying. The coconut macaroons will begin to lose moisture as the machine progressively lowers the temperature.

★ **Keep an eye on the process:** Make sure to periodically monitor the freeze-drying cycle's progress. The time frame might be different, although it might take a day or two. As necessary, adjust the settings.

★ **Verify the Dryness:** Make sure the coconut macaroons that have been freeze-dried are completely dry. Their texture need to be crisp and airy.

★ **Cool Down:** Before handling, let the coconut macaroons that have been freeze-dried come to room temperature.

★ **Keep Safe:** To preserve their crispness, store the freeze-dried coconut macaroons in an airtight receptacle or vacuum-sealed bag.

Advice and Adaptations:

- **Chocolate Dipped (Optional):** For extra taste, dip the bottoms of the freeze-dried coconut macaroons into melted chocolate.
- **Drizzle with Chocolate:** For a decorative touch, drizzle melted chocolate over the tops of the freeze-dried macaroons.
- **Add Almonds or Nuts:** For an extra crunch, stir chopped almonds or other nuts into the coconut mixture.
- **Use Various Extracts:** Try out different extracts, such as coconut or almond, to create interesting flavor combinations.
- **Make Bite-Sized Macaroons:** To make a delicacy that is bite-sized, make smaller macaroons.

13. Best Tasty Fudge Cubes
Ingredients:

- Two cups of chocolate chips (milk, dark, or both)
- One can, or fourteen ounces sweetened condensed milk
- half a cup of butter without salt
- One tsp vanilla essence
- A dash of salt
- Chopped nuts, dried fruit, or flavoring extracts are optional additions.

Tools:

- Saute pan
- Bowl for mixing

- Baking pan that is square
- Paper parchment
- The freezer dryer
- Vacuum pump (should the freeze dryer not have one built in)
- Freeze dryer trays
- Airtight bag or vacuum-sealed container

Making Fudge Cubes:

➢ **Get the baking pan ready:** Using parchment paper, line a square baking pan, providing an overhang for easy removal.

➢ **Melt Ingredients:** Melt chocolate chips, sweetened condensed milk, and unsalted butter in a skillet over low heat, stirring constantly.

➢ **Add the salt and vanilla;** stir until smooth and well blended. Take the liquid from the heat. Add a dash of salt and vanilla extract, and stir.

➢ **Add-Ins Optional:** If preferred, fold in any optional ingredients, such as chopped nuts, dried fruit, or flavoring extracts.

➢ **Switch to Pan:** Evenly spread the fudge mixture in the baking pan that has been prepared.

➢ **Chill:** Put the pan in the fridge and leave it there for the fudge to harden completely, which should take at least two to three hours.

The Freeze-Drying Method:

★ **Setting Up for Freeze Drying:** Before freeze-drying, let the fudge reach room temperature.

★ **How to Fill the Freeze Dryer:** In accordance with the manufacturer's recommendations, preheat the freeze dryer.

★ **Cut into Cubes:** Once the fudge is firm, use the parchment paper overhang to pull it out of the pan. Bite-sized cubes of the fudge should be cut.

★ **Arrange on Trays:** Place the fudge cubes in a uniform layer on the trays of the freeze-dryer.

★ **Establish Freeze Dryer Settings:** Aim for a low temperature of approximately -20°F to -40°F (-29°C to -40°C) for the freeze dryer, and follow the machine's instructions for adjusting the vacuum pressure.

★ **Start the Cycle of Freeze-Drying:** Begin the process of freeze-drying. The machine will progressively lower the temperature and commence the elimination of moisture from the fudge cubes.

★ **Keep an eye on the process:** Make sure to periodically monitor the freeze-drying cycle's progress. The time frame might be different, although it might take a day or two. As necessary, adjust the settings.

★ **Verify the Dryness:** Make sure the fudge cubes that have been freeze-dried are completely dry. Their texture need to be crisp and airy.

★ **Cool Down:** Before handling, let the freeze-dried fudge cubes come to room temperature.

★ **Keep Safe:** Place the freeze-dried fudge cubes in an airtight container or vacuum-sealed bag to keep their crispiness.

Advice and Adaptations:
- **Utilize Various Chocolates:** Try different chocolate flavors to create interesting types of fudge.
- **Layered Fudge:** Pour various chocolate recipes on top of one another to create layered fudge.
- **Sprinkle Sea Salt (Optional):** Before the fudge sets completely, sprinkle it with a small amount of sea salt to create a contrast between sweetness and saltiness.
- **Add Espresso Powder (Optional):** Stir a tiny bit of espresso powder into the fudge mixture to give it a coffee-flavored twist.
- **Dip in White Chocolate (Optional):** Once the fudge cubes have been freeze-dried, coat them with a rich layer of melted white chocolate.

14. Laffy Taffy:
Ingredients
- Two cups of powdered sugar
- one-third cup light corn syrup
- One tablespoon of butter without salt
- One tsp vanilla essence
- 1/4 tsp salt
- (Optional) food coloring
- Concentrated flavor oils or flavor extracts (optional)
- Powdered sugar or cornstarch (for coating)

Tools:

- Saucepan
- A candy thermometer
- Silicone spatula
- Paper parchment
- The freezer dryer
- Vacuum pump (should the freeze dryer not have one built in)
- Freeze dryer trays
- Airtight bag or vacuum-sealed container

How to Prepare Laffy Taffy:

> **Set Up the Work Surface:** Dust a flat surface with powdered sugar or cornstarch after lining it with parchment paper.

> **Mix the ingredients together:** Granulated sugar, light corn syrup, unsalted butter, vanilla extract, and salt should all be combined in a pot. Stir until the sugar melts over a medium heat source.

> **Cook to Soft Ball Stage:** Place a candy thermometer inside the saucepan and cook the mixture until it reaches the soft ball stage, which is approximately 240°F/116°C, while stirring constantly.

> **Include Taste and Color (Optional):** In the final minutes of cooking, if desired, add food coloring and flavor extracts or concentrated flavor oils. To combine, give it a good stir.

- ➤ **Transfer to the Ready Surface:** Transfer the heated taffy mixture onto the surface covered with prepared parchment paper.
- ➤ **Calm A Little Bit:** When the taffy is safe to handle but still warm, let it cool somewhat.
- ➤ **Pull and Stretch:** Continue pulling and stretching the taffy until it is shiny and smooth, using buttered hands or silicone spatulas. Taffy is given a chewy texture and is aerated during this procedure.
- ➤ Roll the taffy into long strips and cut them into bite-sized pieces after shaping them into strips.

The Freeze-Drying Method:

- ★ **Preparation for Freeze Drying:** In order to prepare the Laffy Taffy pieces for freeze-drying, let them cool to room temperature.
- ★ **How to Fill the Freeze Dryer:** In accordance with the manufacturer's recommendations, preheat the freeze dryer.
- ★ **Arrange the Taffy on Trays:** Place the Laffy Taffy pieces in a uniform layer on the freeze-dryer trays.
- ★ **Configure Freeze Dryer Parameters:** Follow the machine's instructions to modify the vacuum pressure and set the temperature to a low range of -20°F to -40°F (-29°C to -40°C).
- ★ **Start the Cycle of Freeze-Drying:** Begin the process of freeze-drying. The Laffy Taffy will begin to lose moisture as the machine progressively lowers the temperature.

★ **Keep an eye on the process:** Make sure to periodically monitor the freeze-drying cycle's progress. The time frame might be different, although it might take a day or two. As necessary, adjust the settings.

★ **Verify the Dryness:** Make sure the Laffy Taffy that has been freeze-dried is completely dry. It ought to be crunchy and airy in texture.

★ **Cool Down:** Before handling, let the freeze-dried Laffy Taffy come to room temperature.

★ **Keep Safe:** To keep the Laffy Taffy crisp, store it in an airtight container or vacuum-sealed bag once it has been freeze-dried.

Advice and Adaptations:

- **Mix Flavors:** Divide the taffy mixture into portions and flavor each one separately to create a variety of flavors.

- **Twist Colors:** To create an eye-catching effect, twist together taffy strips of various colors before cutting.

- **Try Different Extracts:** To create distinctive flavor profiles, try using extracts such as green apple, strawberry, or banana.

- **Roll in Wax Paper:** For a genuine presentation, roll the Laffy Taffy pieces in wax paper after they have freeze-dried.

- **Add Citric Acid (Optional):** During cooking, stir in a tiny bit of citric acid to give it a tart kick.

15. Adorable Nerds

Components:

- 1 cup of sugar, granulated
- 1/4 cup of sugar, powdered
- One-fourth teaspoon of citric acid
- One-fourth teaspoon of baking soda
- 1/4 teaspoon of flavoring essence, such as grape, orange, or strawberry
- food coloring (Optional)
- Cornflour (to dust)

Equipment:

- Bowl for mixing
- Paper parchment
- Small syringe or dropper
- The freezer dryer
- Vacuum pump (should the freeze dryer not have one built in)
- Freeze dryer trays
- Airtight bag or vacuum-sealed container

Nerds Getting ready:

- ➤ **Set Up the Work Surface:** Spread parchment paper on a level surface and sprinkle with cornstarch.
- ➤ **Combine Components:** Mix the powdered sugar, baking soda, citric acid, and granulated sugar in a mixing basin. Blend thoroughly.
- ➤ Add Color and Flavor: Mix the dry mixture with the flavored extract and, if preferred, food

coloring. Perfectly Stir until all of the ingredients are completely incorporated.

➤ **Form Tiny Droplets:** Squeeze or use a small dropper to dispense the sugar mixture into tiny droplets onto the parchment paper. These are the diminutive Nerds.

➤ **Allow to Dry:** Until the Nerds lose their stickiness, let them dry at room temperature for a few hours.

The Freeze-Drying Method:

★ **Getting Ready for Freeze Drying:** Let the Nerds cool fully before freezing and desiccating.

★ **How to Fill the Freeze Dryer:** In accordance with the manufacturer's instructions, preheat the freeze dryer.

★ **Arrange Nerds on Platters:** Place the Nerds in an even layer on the freeze-dryer trays.

★ **Establish Freeze Dryer Settings:** Aim for a low temperature of approximately -20°F to -40°F (-29°C to -40°C) for the freeze dryer, and follow the machine's instructions for adjusting the vacuum pressure.

★ **Start the Cycle of Freeze-Drying:** Begin the process of freeze-drying. The device will begin to gradually reduce the Nerds' temperature and remove moisture from them.

★ **Keep an eye on the process:** Make sure to periodically monitor the freeze-drying cycle's progress. The time frame might be different, although it might take a day or two. As necessary, adjust the settings.

★ **Verify the Dryness:** Make sure the Nerds that have been freeze-dried are completely dry. Their texture ought to be crisp and light.

★ **Cool Down:** Before handling, let the freeze-dried Nerds come to room temperature.

★ **Keep Safe:** Place the freeze-dried Nerds in an airtight container or vacuum-sealed bag to maintain their crispiness.

Advice and Adaptations:

• **Make Up Mixtures of Flavors:** Create a range of combinations by mixing and matching the flavors and colors of your batches of Nerds.

• **Play Around with Shapes:** To create unique Nerd shapes, experiment with different dropper sizes and shapes.

• **Layer Colors:** To create a layered effect, drop Nerds of various colors on top of one another.

• **Add Edible Glitter (Optional):** To give the Nerds a sparkly look, sprinkle edible glitter on them before they completely dry.

• **Mix with Pop Rocks (Optional):** For a crunchy and bubbly treat, mix freeze-dried Nerds with Pop Rocks.

16. Mouthwatering Gummy Bears

Components:

- One cup of fruit juice (pick a flavor, such as raspberry, orange, or cherry)
- 1/4 cup powdered gelatin
- Two tablespoons of maple syrup or honey
- Rubber molds for gummy bears
- Optional: Citric acid (to add a zesty taste)

Tools:

- Saute pan
- Mix the gummy bear molds.
- Syringe or dropper
- The freezer dryer
- Vacuum pump (should the freeze dryer not have one built in)
- Freeze dryer trays
- Airtight bag or vacuum-sealed container

Candy Bears Getting ready:

- ➢ **Get the gummy bear molds ready:** Put the silicone molds for gummy bears on a tray or a level surface.
- ➢ **Mixing the Ingredients:** Put the fruit juice, gelatin powder, and honey/maple syrup into a saucepan. To dissolve the gelatin, thoroughly whisk the mixture.
- ➢ **Heat Gummy Mixture:** Cook, stirring constantly, over low to medium heat until the mixture turns liquid and all of the ingredients are well combined. Keep it from boiling.

➢ **Optional Tangy Flavor:** To achieve a tangy flavor, dissolve the citric acid in the mixture by stirring it in.
➢ **Fill the gummy molds:** Pour the liquid mixture into each cavity of the gummy bear molds using a dropper or syringe.
➢ **Allow to Set:** After the gummy bears are completely firm, let them set in the molds for two to three hours at room temperature.

The Freeze-Drying Method:

★ **Setting Up for Freeze Drying:** Before freeze-drying, let the gummy bears cool completely.
★ **How to Fill the Freeze Dryer:** In accordance with the manufacturer's instructions, preheat the freeze dryer.
★ **Take Gummy Bears Out of the Molds**: When the gummy bears are completely set, carefully remove them from the molds.
★ **Place on Trays:** Using freezer trays, arrange the gummy bears, making sure they are evenly spaced.
★ **Establish Freeze Dryer Settings:** Aim for a low temperature of approximately -20°F to -40°F (-29°C to -40°C) for the freeze dryer, and follow the machine's instructions for adjusting the vacuum pressure.
★ **Start the Cycle of Freeze-Drying:** Begin the process of freeze-drying. The device will start to

gradually reduce the gummy bears' temperature and remove moisture from them.

★ **Keep an eye on the process:** Make sure to periodically monitor the freeze-drying cycle's progress. The time frame might be different, although it might take a day or two. As necessary, adjust the settings.

★ **Verify the Gummy Bears' Dryness:** Make sure the freeze-dried candy is completely dry. Their texture ought to be crisp and light.

★ **Cool Down:** Before handling, let the freeze-dried gummy bears come to room temperature.

★ **How to Store Them:** To keep the gummy bears crisp, store them in an airtight container or vacuum-sealed bag.

Advice and Adaptations:

- **Use Different Juices:** Try making gummy bears with different flavors by experimenting with different fruit juices.

- **Mix Fruit Flavors:** To create interesting flavor combinations, add different fruit juices to the gelatin mixture.

- **Add Vitamin Supplements (Optional):** For an added nutritional boost, think about mixing powdered vitamin supplements into the gummy mixture.

- **Make Bears with Multiple Colors:** Divide the liquid mixture into batches and color them with food coloring. Dust with Powdered Sugar (Optional): For a slightly sweet finish, dust the freeze-dried gummy bears with a light coating of powdered sugar.

17. Flavorful Honeycomb Toffee
Ingredients:
- 1 cup of sugar, granulated
- 1/4 cup of simple corn syrup
- One tsp baking soda
- One tsp vanilla essence
- A dash of salt
- Parchment paper or cooking spray

Tools:
- Saute pan
- Whisk
- Baking sheet
- Paper parchment
- The freezer dryer
- Vacuum pump (should the freeze dryer not have one built in)
- Freeze dryer trays
- Airtight bag or vacuum-sealed container

Making Honeycomb Toffee:
- **Get the baking sheet ready:** A baking sheet can be greased with cooking spray or lined with parchment paper. Put aside.
- **Mix Sugar and Corn Syrup:** In a saucepan set over medium heat, mix light corn syrup and granulated sugar. After the sugar dissolves, stir.

- ➢ **Boil Sugar Mixture:** Without stirring, let the sugar mixture reach a boil. Utilizing a candy thermometer, allow it to attain the hard crack stage of 300°F (149°C).
- ➢ **Add Salt and Baking Soda:** Take the saucepan off of the burner and whisk in the salt, vanilla extract, and baking soda right away. There will be bubbles in the mixture.
- ➢ **Pour onto Baking Sheet:** Quickly and evenly pour the heated toffee mixture onto the baking sheet that has been ready.
- ➢ **Chill and Set:** Give the honeycomb toffee at least one or two hours to cool and set at room temperature.

The Freeze-Drying Method:
- ★ **Setting Up for Freeze Drying:** Before freeze-drying, let the honeycomb toffee cool to room temperature.
- ★ **How to Fill the Freeze Dryer:** In accordance with the manufacturer's instructions, preheat the freeze dryer.
- ★ **Break into Pieces:** Once the honeycomb toffee has fully set, break it into bite-sized pieces.
- ★ **Place on Trays:** Arrange the honeycomb toffee pieces on freeze-dryer trays, ensuring they are evenly spaced.
- ★ **Establish Freeze Dryer Settings:** Aim for a low temperature of approximately -20°F to -40°F (-29°C to -40°C) for the freeze dryer, and follow

the machine's instructions for adjusting the vacuum pressure.

★ **Start the Cycle of Freeze-Drying:** Begin the process of freeze-drying. The machine will gradually lower the temperature and initiate the removal of moisture from the honeycomb toffee.

★ **Keep an eye on the process:** Make sure to periodically monitor the freeze-drying cycle's progress. The time frame might be different, although it might take a day or two. As necessary, adjust the settings.

★ **Check for Dryness:** Ensure that the freeze-dried honeycomb toffee is thoroughly dry. It ought to be crunchy and airy in texture.

★ **Cool Down:** Allow the freeze-dried honeycomb toffee to cool to room temperature before handling.

★ **Keep Safe:** Place the freeze-dried honeycomb toffee in an airtight container or vacuum-sealed bag to maintain its crispiness.

Advice and Adaptations:

● **Add Nuts:** Mix chopped nuts into the toffee mixture for added crunch and flavor.

● **Dip in Chocolate:** After freeze-drying, dip honeycomb toffee pieces in melted chocolate for a delightful coating.

● **Sprinkle Sea Salt (Optional):** Sprinkle a bit of sea salt over the honeycomb toffee before it fully sets for a sweet and salty contrast.

- **Break into Bark:** Instead of breaking the toffee into small pieces, leave it in larger sheets to create a toffee bark.
- **Gift Idea:** Package the freeze-dried honeycomb toffee in decorative bags or boxes for a homemade gift.

18. Lovely Jellied Candy
Components:
- 2 cups fruit juice (orange, raspberry, or any desired flavor)
- 1/4 cup powdered gelatin
- 1/2 cup honey or maple syrup (adjust to taste)
- 1-2 tablespoons lemon juice (for tartness, optional)
- Cooking oil or cooking spray

Tools:
- Saute pan
- Whisk
- Candy thermometer
- Gummy molds or silicone molds
- The freezer dryer
- Vacuum pump (should the freeze dryer not have one built in)
- Freeze dryer trays
- Airtight bag or vacuum-sealed container

<u>Jellied Candy Preparation:</u>
- ➤ **Prepare Molds:** Grease gummy molds or silicone molds lightly with cooking oil or use cooking spray. Put aside.
- ➤ **Bloom Gelatin:** In a small bowl, mix gelatin powder with a small amount of cold water. Let it bloom while preparing the fruit juice mixture.
- ➤ **Warm Fruit Juice:** In a saucepan, heat the fruit juice over low to medium heat. Do not bring it to a boil; aim for a warm but not scalding temperature.
- ➤ **Add Honey or Maple Syrup:** Stir in honey or maple syrup to the warm fruit juice, ensuring it dissolves completely.
- ➤ **Add Bloomed Gelatin:** Add the bloomed gelatin to the fruit juice mixture, stirring continuously until the gelatin is fully dissolved.
- ➤ **Add Lemon Juice (Optional):** If a slightly tart flavor is desired, add lemon juice to the mixture and stir well.
- ➤ **Pour into Molds:** Pour the jellied candy mixture into the prepared molds, ensuring they are filled to the top.
- ➤ **Set in the Refrigerator:** Place the molds in the refrigerator and allow the jellied candy to set for at least 2-3 hours or until firm.

The Freeze-Drying Method:
- ★ **Getting Ready for Freeze Drying:** Allow the jellied candy to cool to room temperature before freeze-drying.

★ **How to Fill the Freeze Dryer:** In accordance with the manufacturer's instructions, preheat the freeze dryer.

★ **Take from Molds:** After the jellied candy has completely set, carefully take it from the molds.

★ **Place on Trays:** Using freeze-dryer trays, place the jellied candy pieces, making sure they are uniformly spaced.

★ **Establish Freeze Dryer Settings:** Aim for a low temperature of approximately -20°F to -40°F (-29°C to -40°C) for the freeze dryer, and follow the machine's instructions for adjusting the vacuum pressure.

★ **Start the Cycle of Freeze-Drying:** Begin the process of freeze-drying. The jellied candy will begin to lose moisture as the machine progressively lowers the temperature.

★ **Keep an eye on the process:** Make sure to periodically monitor the freeze-drying cycle's progress. The time frame might be different, although it might take a day or two. As necessary, adjust the settings.

★ **Check for Dryness:** Verify that the freeze-dried jellied candy is completely dry by checking its dryness. It ought to be crunchy and airy in texture.

★ **Cool Down:** Before handling, let the freeze-dried jellied candy come to room temperature.

★ **Keep Safe:** To keep the freeze-dried jellied candy crisp, store it in an airtight jar or vacuum-sealed bag.

Advice and Adaptations:

- **Layered Candy:** To make multi-layered jelly beans, let each layer solidify completely before proceeding to the next.
- **Use Different Molds:** To create an aesthetically pleasing collection, try different mold shapes and sizes.
- **Mix Fruit Juices:** To produce interesting flavor combinations, combine various fruit juices.
- **Dust with granulated sugar (Optional):** For a sweet touch, dust the freeze-dried jellied candy with powdered sugar.
- **Present Idea:** Present the freeze-dried jellied candies in attractive bags to make a charming handcrafted present.

19. Irresistible Nut and Fruit Clusters
Ingredients:

- One cup of mixed nuts, (any combination of pecans, walnuts, and almonds)
- Half a cup of dried fruits, such as raisins, apricots, or cranberries, if preferred
- Half a cup of maple syrup or honey
- One tsp vanilla essence
- Half a teaspoon of cinnamon, if desired
- A dash of salt

Tools:

- Bowl for mixing
- Saute pan

- Baking sheet
- Paper parchment
- The freezer dryer
- Vacuum pump (should the freeze dryer not have one built in)
- Freeze dryer trays
- Airtight bag or vacuum-sealed container

Preparing Fruit and Nut Clusters:

- ➢ **Warm up the oven:** Set the oven temperature to 350°F (177°C).
- ➢ **Toast Nuts:** Arrange the mixed nuts on a baking sheet and bake them for 8 to 10 minutes, or until they begin to turn a light golden color. Let them cool.
- ➢ **Dried Fruits Should Be Chopped:** Cut huge dried fruits into bite-sized pieces.
- ➢ **Mix Nuts and Fruits:** Place chopped dry fruits and toasted nuts in a mixing bowl.
- ➢ **Preparing Honey Mixture:** To make the honey mixture, place the honey or maple syrup in a pot and cook it over medium heat. Add a small amount of salt, vanilla essence, and cinnamon (if using). Heat the mixture until it starts to flow a little bit.
- ➢ **Coat Fruits and Nuts:** Drizzle the blended fruits and nuts with the honey mixture. To ensure even coating, stir thoroughly.
- ➢ **Create Groups:** Use parchment paper to line a baking sheet. Scoop some of the mixture with a spoon to create clusters on the sheet.

➣ **Set at Room Temperature:** Give the clusters a minimum of one to two hours to set at room temperature, or until they are firm to the touch.

The Freeze-Drying Method:
  ★ **Getting Ready for Freeze Drying:** Before freeze-drying, let the fruit and nut clusters cool to room temperature.
  ★ **How to Fill the Freeze Dryer:** In accordance with the manufacturer's recommendations, preheat the freeze dryer.
  ★ **Arrange Groups on Trays:** Place the nut and fruit clusters in an equal layer on the freeze-dryer trays.
  ★ **Establish Freeze Dryer Settings:** Aim for a low temperature of approximately -20°F to -40°F (-29°C to -40°C) for the freeze dryer, and follow the machine's instructions for adjusting the vacuum pressure.
  ★ **Start the Cycle of Freeze-Drying:** Begin the process of freeze-drying. The machine will start to progressively reduce the temperature and start to extract moisture from the clusters of fruit and nuts.
  ★ **Keep an eye on the process:** Make sure to periodically monitor the freeze-drying cycle's progress. The time frame might be different, although it might take a day or two. As necessary, adjust the settings.
  ★ **Check Dryness:** Verify the fruit and nut clusters that have been freeze-dried to make sure they

are completely dry. Their texture need to be crisp and airy.

★ **Cool Down:** Before handling, let the freeze-dried fruit and nut clusters come to room temperature.

★ **Keep Safe:** To preserve the crispness of the freeze-dried fruit and nut clusters, store them in an airtight container or vacuum-sealed bag.

Advice and Adaptations:

- **Add Chocolate, if Choosing to:** For a luxurious touch, dip or drizzle the freeze-dried clusters with melted chocolate.
- **Try Different Spices:** To improve the flavor profile, try experimenting with different spices such as cardamom, cloves, or nutmeg.
- **Use Raw or Roasted Nuts:** If you'd like a different flavor profile, you can use either raw or roasted nuts.
- **Form Bite-Sized Groups:** Cut into smaller clusters for an easy-to-transport snack.
- **Mix Seeds:** For extra crunch, add seeds like sunflower or pumpkin seeds.

20. Delish Peanut Butter Cups
Components:

- One cup of smooth peanut butter
- Half a cup of powdered sugar
- 1/4 cup melted unsalted butter
- Half a teaspoon of extract from vanilla
- A dash of salt

- Two cups fine chocolate, chopped (dark, milk, or a mixture
- Chocolate molds or cooking spray

Tools:
- Bowl for mixing
- Double boiler or perhaps a bowl safe for the microwave
- Utensil or spatula
- Mini cupcake liners or chocolate molds
- The freezer dryer
- Vacuum pump (should the freeze dryer not have one built in)
- Freeze dryer trays
- Airtight bag or vacuum-sealed container

Cups with peanut butter Getting ready:
- ➤ **Get the peanut butter filling ready:** Melted unsalted butter, powdered sugar, vanilla essence, creamy peanut butter, and a dash of salt should all be combined in a mixing dish. Blend until well combined.
- ➤ **Melt Chocolate:** Use a microwave or double boiler to melt the premium chocolate. Mix until completely melted and smooth.
- ➤ **Get the chocolate molds ready:** Lightly mist the small cupcake liners or chocolate molds with cooking spray.
- ➤ **Coat Molds with Chocolate:** Spoon a tiny amount of melted chocolate into each mold, ensuring the bottom and sides are coated

equally. To distribute the chocolate, use the back of the spoon.

➤ **Incorporate the peanut butter filling:** Leaving space at the top, spoon a heaping portion of peanut butter filling into each chocolate-coated mold.

➤ **Cover with Chocolate:** Pour additional melted chocolate over the peanut butter filling to completely cover it, then use a spatula to smooth the top.

➤ **Tap and Set:** To ensure an equal surface and get rid of air bubbles, lightly tap the molds on the counter. Refrigerate the peanut butter cups for a minimum of two hours to allow them to firm.

The Freeze-Drying Method:

★ **Getting Ready for Freeze-Drying:** Before freeze-drying, let the peanut butter cups cool to room temperature.

★ **How to Fill the Freeze Dryer:** In accordance with the manufacturer's recommendations, preheat the freeze dryer.

★ **Remove from Molds:** After the peanut butter cups are completely set, carefully take them out of the molds.

★ **Arrange on Trays:** Place the peanut butter cups on the trays of the freeze-dryer, making sure that they are evenly apart.

★ **Establish Freeze Dryer Settings:** Aim for a low temperature of approximately -20°F to -40°F (-29°C to -40°C) for the freeze dryer, and follow

the machine's instructions for adjusting the vacuum pressure.

★ **Start the Cycle of Freeze-Drying:** Begin the process of freeze-drying. The device will begin to gradually reduce the peanut butter cups' temperature and remove moisture from them.

★ **Keep an eye on the process:** Make sure to periodically monitor the freeze-drying cycle's progress. The time frame might be different, although it might take a day or two. As necessary, adjust the settings.

★ **Verify the Dryness:** Make sure the peanut butter cups are completely dry after being freeze-dried. Their texture need to be crisp and airy.

★ **Cool Down:** Before handling, let the freeze-dried peanut butter cups come to room temperature.

★ **Keep Safe:** To preserve their crispness, store the freeze-dried peanut butter cups in an airtight receptacle or vacuum-sealed bag.

Advice and Adaptations:
- **Use a Different Kind of Chocolate:** Try different kinds of chocolate, like milk, white, or dark, to create interesting flavor combinations.
- **Add Crunch:** To add texture to the peanut butter filling, mix chopped nuts, crushed pretzels, or crispy rice cereal.
- **Sprinkle Sea Salt (Optional):** Before the peanut butter cups completely set, sprinkle some sea

salt on top to create a contrast between sweetness and saltiness.

- **Make Mini Cups:** For bite-sized treats, make smaller peanut butter cups.
- **Drizzle with Chocolate (Optional):** For a decorative touch, pour a little more melted chocolate over the peanut butter cups after they have freeze-dried.

21. Mouthwatering Fruit Popsicles
Ingredients:
- Two cups of fruit, frozen or fresh (mango, pineapple, berries, or any other fruit you like)
- ¼ cup maple syrup or honey, adjusted to taste
- One tablespoon of optionally tart lemon juice
- one cup coconut water or water
- Sticks and molds for popsicles

Tools:
- Blender
- Saute pan
- Whisk Popsicle sticks and molds
- The freezer dryer
- Vacuum pump (should the freeze dryer not have one built in)
- Freeze dryer trays
- Airtight bag or vacuum-sealed container

Fruit Popsicles Preparation:
- ➢ **Get the Fruit Ready:** Wash and chop fresh fruit or thaw frozen fruit if using. Ensure the pieces

are bite-sized and suitable for the popsicle molds.

➢ **Blend Fruit:** In a blender, combine the fruit, honey or maple syrup, and water or coconut water. Blend until smooth. Add lemon juice if you desire a slightly tart flavor.

➢ **Strain (Optional):** For a smoother popsicle texture, strain the blended mixture through a fine mesh sieve to remove any seeds or pulp.

➢ **Fill Popsicle Molds:** Pour the blended fruit mixture into popsicle molds, leaving a small gap at the top to accommodate expansion.

➢ **Insert Sticks:** Place popsicle sticks into the molds, ensuring they are secure in the center of each Popsicle.

➢ **Freeze:** Freeze the popsicles for at least 4-6 hours or until completely solid.

The Freeze-Drying Method:

★ **Setting Up for Freeze Drying:** Allow the fruit popsicles to thaw slightly to ease removal from the molds before freeze-drying.

★ **Load the Freeze Dryer:** Preheat the freeze dryer according to the manufacturer's instructions.

★ **Remove from Molds:** Carefully remove the fruit popsicles from the molds once they are partially thawed.

★ **Place on Trays:** Arrange the popsicles on freeze-dryer trays, ensuring they are evenly spaced.

★ **Establish Freeze Dryer Settings:** Aim for a low temperature of approximately -20°F to -40°F (-29°C to -40°C) for the freeze dryer, and follow the machine's instructions for adjusting the vacuum pressure.

★ **Start the Cycle of Freeze-Drying:** Begin the process of freeze-drying. The machine will gradually lower the temperature and initiate the removal of moisture from the popsicles.

★ **Keep an eye on the process:** Make sure to periodically monitor the freeze-drying cycle's progress. The time frame might be different, although it might take a day or two. As necessary, adjust the settings.

★ **Verify the Dryness:** Ensure that the freeze-dried fruit popsicles are thoroughly dry. Their texture need to be crisp and airy.

★ **Cool Down:** Allow the freeze-dried fruit popsicles to cool to room temperature before handling.

★ **Keep Safe:** Place the freeze-dried fruit popsicles in an airtight container or vacuum-sealed bag to maintain their crispiness.

Advice and Adaptations:
- **Mix Fruit Flavors:** Create multi-flavored popsicles by blending different fruits together.
- **Layered Popsicles:** Freeze the blended mixtures in layers for a visually appealing and colorful popsicle.

- **Add Coconut Milk:** Enhance the creaminess by adding coconut milk to the fruit blend before freezing.
- **Dip in Chocolate (Optional):** After freeze-drying, dip the tips of the fruit popsicles in melted chocolate for a decadent touch.
- **Sprinkle Coconut Shreds (Optional):** Sprinkle coconut shreds over the freeze-dried popsicles for added texture.

22. Tasty DIY Chocolate-Covered Strawberries
Components:
- Strawberry fresh
- Eight ounces, or 227 grams, of fine chocolate (dark, milk, or white)
- Optional garnishes (shredded coconut, chopped almonds, and sprinkles)

Tools:
- Double boiler or perhaps a bowl safe for the microwave
- Baking sheet
- Paper parchment
- Sticks or toothpicks
- The freezer dryer
- Vacuum pump (should the freeze dryer not have one built in)
- Freeze dryer trays
- Airtight bag or vacuum-sealed container

Strawberries Covered with Chocolate Getting ready:

- ➢ **Choose Fresh Strawberries:** Select ripe, fresh strawberries with unbroken green stalks. Use a paper towel to pat them dry after rinsing.
- ➢ **Prepare Toppings (Optional):** If you choose to use toppings, prepare them in separate dishes and set them away, such as chopped almonds or shredded coconut.
- ➢ **Melt the Chocolate:** To melt the chocolate, use a microwave-safe bowl or a double boiler. Blend until a smooth consistency is achieved. Be cautious not to overheat, as chocolate can burn.
- ➢ **Dip the Strawberries:** Holding a strawberry by its stem, carefully dip it into the molten chocolate, making sure to coat it completely. Let the dripping chocolate fall off.
- ➢ **Add Toppings (Optional):** Roll the strawberry coated in chocolate in your preferred topping right away, while the chocolate is still wet, if you plan to use it.
- ➢ **Put this on parchment paper:** Place every strawberry wrapped in chocolate on a baking sheet covered with parchment paper. Carefully make sure they are not in contact.
- ➢ **Put it away and chill:** Let the strawberries covered in chocolate cool and settle to room temperature. If you put them in the refrigerator for about fifteen minutes, you can expedite the process.
- ➢ **Place toothpicks or skewers:** Gently in the middle of each strawberry that has been covered

with chocolate. This will facilitate their handling during the freeze-drying process.

The Freeze-Drying Method:

★ **Getting Ready for Freeze Drying:** After preparing the chocolate-covered strawberries, let them cool to room temperature and then freeze-dry them.

★ **How to Fill the Freeze Dryer:** In accordance with the manufacturer's recommendations, preheat the freeze dryer.

★ **Arrange Trays of Strawberries:** As you arrange the chocolate-covered strawberries on the freeze-dryer trays, make sure they are not touching and are spaced evenly apart.

★ **Establish Freeze Dryer Settings:** Aim for a low temperature of approximately -20°F to -40°F (-29°C to -40°C) for the freeze dryer, and follow the machine's instructions for adjusting the vacuum pressure.

★ **Start the Cycle of Freeze-Drying:** Begin the process of freeze-drying. The chocolate-covered strawberries will begin to lose moisture as the machine progressively reduces the temperature.

★ **Keep an eye on the process:** Make sure to periodically monitor the freeze-drying cycle's progress. The time frame might be different, although it might take a day or two. As necessary, adjust the settings.

★ **Verify the Dryness:** Ensure that the freeze-dried chocolate-covered strawberries are absolutely dry. They ought to be crisp in texture.

★ **Cool Down:** Let the freeze-dried strawberries come down to room temperature before interacting with them.

★ **Take out of the trays:** Remove the strawberries wrapped in chocolate that has been freeze-dried carefully from the trays.

★ **Keep Safe:** To preserve their crispness, store the freeze-dried strawberries in an airtight jar or vacuum-sealed bag.

Advice and Adaptations:

- **Try Something with Chocolate:** Try dark, milk, or white chocolate for distinct flavor qualities.
- **Variety of Toppings:** To enhance texture and eye appeal, experiment with different toppings like chopped almonds, shredded coconut, or colorful sprinkles.
- **Suggestion for a Gift:** Put the strawberries covered in chocolate that has been freeze-dried inside a pretty box to make a lovely homemade present.
- **Serve Chilled:** Enjoy these freeze-dried goodies chilled, right from the freezer.

23. The Best Indulgent Fruit Leather

Ingredients:
- Four cups of ripe fruit (apples, peaches, strawberries, or a combination)
- One tablespoon of optionally sour lemon juice
- One to two teaspoons of maple syrup or honey (optional, for sweetness)

Tools:
- Food processor or blender
- Peel-and-stick baking sheets or parchment paper
- Oven or dehydrator
- The freezer dryer
- Vacuum pump (should the freeze dryer not have one built in)
- Freeze dryer trays
- Airtight bag or vacuum-sealed container

How to Prepare Fruit Leather:
- ➢ **Choose and Cut Fruit:** Select juicy, delicious fruits. Clean, peel (if necessary), and take out any seeds or pits. Chop the fruit coarsely.
- ➢ **Mix the Fruit:** Puree the fruit in a food processor or blender until it's smooth. To improve flavor, add lemon juice and sugar, if using.
- ➢ **Strain (Optional):** To remove the pulp and seeds from the fruit puree, pass it through a fine-mesh sieve for a smoother texture.
- ➢ **Get the oven or dehydrator ready:** Set your oven to the lowest setting (typically about 140°F

or 60°C) or preheat your dehydrator to 135°F (57°C).

➢ **Distribute on the Dehydrator Sheets:** Use parchment paper or non-stick sheets to line the dehydrator trays. Transfer the fruit puree onto the liners, leveling it out to a thickness of approximately 1/8 inch.

➢ **Dehydrate:** Use a dehydrator for 6–8 hours or an oven for 8–12 hours to dehydrate the fruit puree. Cut into Strips: After the fruit leather has dried, cut it into the desired shapes or into strips. Test for doneness by sticking your finger in the center; it should feel tacky but not sticky.

The Freeze-Drying Method:

★ **Getting Ready for Freeze Drying:** Allow the fruit leather strips to cool to room temperature before freeze-drying.

★ **How to Fill the Freeze Dryer:** In accordance with the manufacturer's recommendations, preheat the freeze dryer.

★ **Put Strips in Order on Trays:** Arrange the fruit leather strips so that they are not touching and are evenly spaced out on the freeze-dryer trays.

★ **Establish Freeze Dryer Settings:** Aim for a low temperature of approximately -20°F to -40°F (-29°C to -40°C) for the freeze dryer, and follow the machine's instructions for adjusting the vacuum pressure.

★ **Start the Cycle of Freeze-Drying:** Begin the process of freeze-drying. The device will start the process of removing moisture from the fruit leather and progressively reduce the temperature.

★ **Keep an eye on the process:** Make sure to periodically monitor the freeze-drying cycle's progress. The time frame might be different, although it might take a day or two. As necessary, adjust the settings.

★ **Check For Dryness:** Verify the fruit leather that has been freeze-dried to make sure it is completely dry. It need to be crisp in texture.

★ **Cool Down:** Before handling, let the fruit leather that has been freeze-dried come to room temperature.

★ **Remove from Trays:** The freeze-dried fruit leather should be carefully taken out of the trays.

★ **Keep Safe:** To preserve its crispness, store the freeze-dried fruit leather in a vacuum-sealed bag or airtight container.

Advice and Adaptations:

- **Combine Fruits:** Combine several fruits to create interesting concoctions with a range of flavors.
- **Spices:** You can improve the flavor of the fruit puree by adding a dash of nutmeg, cinnamon, or other spices.
- **Custom Shapes:** To make interesting and eye-catching shapes for the fruit leather, use cookie cutters.

- **Roll for Fruit Rolls:** To make fruit rolls, roll the fruit leather strips. These provide a quick and portable snack.
- **Try Out Some Sweeteners:** Investigate different sweeteners, such as concentrated fruit juice or agave nectar.

24. Delectable Homemade Caramel
Ingredients:
- 1 cup of sugar, granulated
- Half a cup of butter without salt
- Half a cup of heavy cream
- One tsp vanilla essence
- A dash of salt

Tools:
- Saute pan
- A candy thermometer
- Whisk
- Paper parchment
- The freezer dryer
- Vacuum pump (should the freeze dryer not have one built in)
- Freeze dryer trays
- Airtight bag or vacuum-sealed container

How to Prepare Caramel:
- ➢ **Get the ingredients ready:** To make the caramel, first measure out all of the ingredients.
- ➢ **Melt Sugar:** Melt the granulated sugar in a pot over medium heat, whisking all the time.

Continue until the sugar turns into an amber liquid that is smooth.

➤ **Put in the butter:** Gently stir in the unsalted butter and continue to whisk until the butter is well combined with the melted sugar.

➤ **Pour in Heavy Cream:** Whisk continuously while slowly adding the heavy cream. Be extra cautious as the mixture will bubble.

➤ **Proceed Cooking:** Place a candy thermometer inside the saucepan and cook the caramel mixture until it reaches the soft-ball stage, which is 240°F (116°C).

➤ **Add Vanilla and Salt:** Take the saucepan off of the burner and mix in a small amount of salt and vanilla extract. Blend until thoroughly blended.

➤ **Calm A Little Bit:** Before processing any further, let the caramel cool somewhat so that it becomes thicker.

The Freeze-Drying Method:

★ **Getting ready for Freeze-Drying:** Before freezing-drying the caramel, let it cool to room temperature.

★ **How to Fill the Freeze Dryer:** In accordance with the manufacturer's recommendations, preheat the freeze dryer.

★ **On parchment paper, spread out:** Place parchment paper inside the trays of freeze-dryers. Transfer the caramel onto the parchment paper and distribute it thinly, evenly.

★ **Establish Freeze Dryer Settings:** Aim for a low temperature of approximately -20°F to -40°F (-29°C to -40°C) for the freeze dryer, and follow the machine's instructions for adjusting the vacuum pressure.

★ **Start the Cycle of Freeze-Drying:** Begin the process of freeze-drying. The device will start to gently reduce the temperature and remove the moisture from the caramel.

★ **Keep an eye on the process:** Make sure to periodically monitor the freeze-drying cycle's progress. The time frame might be different, although it might take a day or two. As necessary, adjust the settings.

★ **Verify the Dryness:** Make sure the caramel that has been freeze-dried is completely dry. It need to be crisp in texture.

★ **Cool Down:** Before handling, let the caramel that has been freeze-dried come to room temperature.

★ **Break into Pieces:** Once the caramel has completely dried, split it up into bite-sized pieces with a fork.

★ **Keep Safe:** To preserve its crispness, store the freeze-dried caramel in an airtight jar or vacuum-sealed bag.

Advice and Adaptations:

• **Try Experimenting with Flavor:** For a salted caramel, add a small amount of sea salt, or use other flavorings such as nutmeg or cinnamon.

- **Add Nuts:** Toss in chopped almonds or pecans for a delicious crunch.
- **Dip in Chocolate:** For a sumptuous treat, dip the caramel pieces in melted chocolate after they have been freeze-dried.
- **To make caramel powder:** To make a powder to use as a topping for drinks or desserts, crush the freeze-dried caramel.

25. Fruit-Based Delicious Gummies

Components:
- Two cups of fruit, frozen or fresh (mangos, berries, or any other fruit you want)
- One-fourth cup water
- 1/4 cup maple syrup or honey
- 1/4 cup powdered gelatin
- One tablespoon of optionally sour lemon juice

Tools:
- Blender
- Saute pan
- Whisk
- Silicone molds or gummy molds
- The freezer dryer
- Vacuum pump (should the freeze dryer not have one built in)
- Freeze dryer trays
- Airtight bag or vacuum-sealed container

Gummies Made with Fruit Getting ready:

> **Select and Cut Fruit:** Choose your preferred fruit, either fresh or frozen. As necessary, wash and prep them.

> **Mix the Fruit:** Puree the fruit in a blender until it's smooth. For a smoother texture, strain the puree through a fine mesh screen to get rid of the pulp and seeds.

> **Prepare Gelatin Mixture:** To make the gelatin mixture, put the water, honey (or maple syrup), and gelatin powder in a pot. Give it a few minutes to settle so the gelatin can bloom.

> **Heat Gelatin Mixture:** Stir the mixture continuously over low heat until the gelatin dissolves completely. Take off the heat.

> **Mix Fruit Puree:** Gently whisk the fruit puree into the gelatin mixture after adding it. If you would like a somewhat tart flavor, add some lemon juice.

> **Pour into Molds:** Transfer the fruit-gelatin blend into silicone or gummy molds. To eliminate air bubbles, lightly tap the molds.

> **Put in the Refrigerator:** After the molds are placed in the refrigerator, the gummies should firm up after at least two to three hours.

Procedure for Freeze-Drying:

★ **Setting Up for Freeze Drying:** Before freeze-drying, let the fruit-based gummies cool to room temperature.

★ **How to Fill the Freeze Dryer:** In accordance with the manufacturer's recommendations, preheat the freeze dryer.

★ **Arrange candies on trays:** Make sure the fruit-based gummies are not touching and are uniformly spaced out on the freeze-dryer trays.

★ **Establish Freeze Dryer Settings:** Aim for a low temperature of approximately -20°F to -40°F (-29°C to -40°C) for the freeze dryer, and follow the machine's instructions for adjusting the vacuum pressure.

★ **Start the Cycle of Freeze-Drying:** Begin the process of freeze-drying. The device will start to gently reduce the gummies' temperature and remove moisture from them.

★ **Keep an eye on the process:** Make sure to periodically monitor the freeze-drying cycle's progress. The time frame might be different, although it might take a day or two. As necessary, adjust the settings.

★ **Verify the Dryness:** Make sure the fruit-based gummies that have been freeze-dried are completely dry. They ought to be crisp in texture.

★ **Cool Down:** Before handling, let the freeze-dried gummies come to room temperature.

★ **Remove from Trays:** The freeze-dried fruit-based gummies should be carefully taken out of the trays.

★ **Keep Safe:** To keep the freeze-dried gummies crisp, store them in an airtight jar or vacuum-sealed bag.

Advice and Adaptations:

- **Blend Fruit Tastes:** Try combining different fruits to create a range of flavors.
- **Coat in Sugar (Optional):** After freeze-drying, sprinkle the gummies in a little powdered sugar for a candy-like finish.
- **Add a Vitamin C Boost:** To increase nutritional value, include fruits high in vitamin C or take a vitamin C supplement.
- **Make Forms:** To make gummies in a variety of shapes, select entertaining and creative molds.
- **Mix with Additional Snacks:** For a delicious combination, combine fruit-based freeze-dried candies with other freeze-dried treats.

26. Sweet Homemade Marshmallows

Components:

- Three teaspoons of plain gelatin
- Half a cup of cold water (for gelatin to bloom)
- Two cups of powdered sugar
- Water, half a cup (for sugar syrup)
- Half a cup of light corn syrup
- 1/4 tsp salt
- Two tsp of essence from vanilla
- Sugar in powder form, for dusting

Tools:

- Attached whisk with stand mixer
- Saute pan
- A candy thermometer

- Paper parchment
- Baking dish
- The freezer dryer
- Vacuum pump (should the freeze dryer not have one built in)
- Freeze dryer trays
- Airtight bag or vacuum-sealed container

The Making of Marshmallows:

- ➤ **Get the gelatin ready:** Place the gelatin and 1/2 cup of cold water in the bowl of a stand mixer. While you make the sugar syrup, let it bloom.
- ➤ **To make sugar syrup:** Granulated sugar, 1/2 cup water, corn syrup, and salt should all be combined in a pot. Fit the pot with a candy thermometer.
- ➤ **Heat Sugar Mixture:** Heat the mixture until it reaches the soft-ball stage, which is 240°F (116°C), over medium heat.
- ➤ **Whip Gelatin:** Begin whipping the gelatin at a low speed while the sugar syrup is cooking.
- ➤ **Pour Sugar Syrup:** With the mixer running, gradually pour the sugar syrup into the whipped gelatin after it reaches 240°F (116°C). Be cautious as the mixture will be heated.
- ➤ **Boost Speed:** Turn up the mixer to its highest setting and beat the mixture until it gets shiny, thick, and forms stiff peaks. Usually, this takes ten to fifteen minutes.
- ➤ **Add Vanilla Extract:** To incorporate, add the vanilla extract and beat for an extra minute.

- ➤ **Get the baking dish ready:** With an overhang on the sides, line a baking dish with parchment paper. Sprinkle the parchment with granulated sugar.
- ➤ **Pour and Set:** Evenly distribute the marshmallow mixture into the dish that has been prepared. Add a little extra powdered sugar on top.
- ➤ **Placed at Room Temperature:** Until the marshmallows are completely solid, let them sit at room temperature for at least six hours or overnight.

The Freeze-Drying Method:
- ★ **Getting Ready for Freeze Drying:** Before freeze-drying, let the marshmallows cool to room temperature.
- ★ **How to Fill the Freeze Dryer:** In accordance with the manufacturer's recommendations, preheat the freeze dryer.
- ★ **Cut Marshmallows:** Using the overhanging parchment paper, carefully remove the marshmallow block from the baking dish. Shape the marshmallows into the forms you like.
- ★ **Place on Trays:** Using a freeze-dryer tray, place the marshmallow pieces in a uniform layer.
- ★ **Establish Freeze Dryer Settings:** Aim for a low temperature of approximately -20°F to -40°F (-29°C to -40°C) for the freeze dryer, and follow the machine's instructions for adjusting the vacuum pressure.

★ **Start the Cycle of Freeze-Drying:** Begin the process of freeze-drying. The device will start to gently reduce the marshmallows' temperature and remove moisture from them.

★ **Keep an eye on the process:** Make sure to periodically monitor the freeze-drying cycle's progress. The time frame might be different, although it might take a day or two. As necessary, adjust the settings.

★ **Verify the Dryness:** Make sure the marshmallows that have been freeze-dried are completely dry. Their texture need to be crisp and airy.

★ **Cool Down:** Before handling, let the freeze-dried marshmallows come to room temperature.

★ **Keep Safe:** To preserve their crispness, store the freeze-dried marshmallows in an airtight receptacle or vacuum-sealed bag.

Advice and Adaptations:

● **Taste-Aware Marshmallows:** For flavored marshmallows, whisk in flavor extracts, such as peppermint or almond extract.

● **Colored Marshmallows:** For a lively and vibrant variation, add food coloring to the marshmallow mixture.

● **Chocolate Dipped (Optional):** For a delectable covering, dip freeze-dried marshmallows into melted chocolate.

● **Use Cookie Cutters:** To add a festive touch, use cookie cutters to cut marshmallows into shapes.

- **Make Marshmallow Sandwiches:** To make marshmallow sandwiches, sandwich two pieces of marshmallow between a layer of chocolate.

27. The Tastiest Junior Mints
Recipes:
Mint Filling Ingredients:
- One cup of sugar powder
- Two teaspoons softened unsalted butter
- Half a teaspoon of extract from peppermint
- One spoonful of heavy cream

Regarding the coating of chocolate:
- One cup of chips with dark chocolate
- One tablespoon of coconut oil

Tools:
- Bowl for mixing
- Piping bag or little spoon
- Paper parchment
- The freezer dryer
- Vacuum pump (should the freeze dryer not have one built in)
- Freeze dryer trays
- Airtight bag or vacuum-sealed container

How to Prepare Mint Filling:
- ➢ **Get the mint filling ready**: Beat together powdered sugar, softened butter, heavy cream, and peppermint essence in a mixing dish. Blend until a silky, workable consistency is reached.

➢ **Form Mint Centers:** On a tray lined with parchment paper, shape small, round mint centers using a piping bag or a small spoon. Be sure to bite them small.
➢ **Freeze or Chill:** Put the tray with the mint centers in the refrigerator or freezer for a few hours, or until they solidify.

Process of Freeze-Drying and Chocolate Coating:
★ **To make the chocolate coating:** Place dark chocolate chips and coconut oil in a bowl that is safe to microwave and stir until smooth.
★ **Coat the Mint Centers:** Make sure the chocolate has completely covered each frozen or cooled mint center by dipping it into it. Let the dripping chocolate fall off.
★ **Put on Trays for Freezing Dryers:** Arrange the chocolate-covered mint centers so they are not pressed together on the freeze-dryer trays.
★ **Warm up the freeze dryer:** In accordance with the manufacturer's recommendations, preheat the freeze dryer.
★ **Establish Freeze Dryer Settings:** Aim for a low temperature of approximately -20°F to -40°F (-29°C to -40°C) for the freeze dryer, and follow the machine's instructions for adjusting the vacuum pressure.
★ **Start the Freeze-Drying Cycle:** The freeze-drying procedure should be started. The device will start to gradually reduce the

temperature and remove moisture from the centers of the mints coated in chocolate.

★ **Keep an eye on the process:** Make sure to periodically monitor the freeze-drying cycle's progress. The time frame might be different, although it might take a day or two. As necessary, adjust the settings.

★ **Verify the Dryness:** Make sure the chocolate-covered mint centers that have been freeze-dried are completely dry. Their texture need to be crisp and airy.

★ **Cool Down:** Before handling, let the freeze-dried Junior Mints come to room temperature.

★ **Keep Safe:** To preserve their crispness, store the freeze-dried Junior Mints in an airtight receptacle or vacuum-sealed bag.

Advice and Adaptations:

- **Modify Peppermint Extract (Optional):** Change the amount of peppermint extract to suit your taste preferences for a stronger mint flavor.
- **Add Food Coloring (Optional):** To achieve a classic Junior Mints look, mix in a few drops of green food coloring to the mint filling.
- **Try Different Chocolate (Optional):** To create a variety of flavor profiles, try experimenting with different chocolate varieties, such as milk chocolate or white chocolate.
- **Serve Chilled (Optional):** For a cool and revitalizing treat, consume the freeze-dried Junior Mints straight out of the fridge.

- **Present Boxes:** For a charming homemade gift, present the freeze-dried Junior Mints in attractive bags or boxes.

28. Mouth-watering Salt Water Taffy:

Ingredients:
- Two cups of powdered sugar
- One cup of light corn syrup
- One tablespoon of butter without salt
- one cup of water
- two tsp cornstarch
- One tsp salt
- One teaspoon glycerin (for texture only, optional)
- Extracts of flavors (such as fruit tastes, peppermint, and vanilla)
- food coloring(Optional)
- Sugar in powder form (for dusting)

Tools:
- Saute pan
- A candy thermometer
- Wooden spoon
- Paper parchment
- The freezer dryer
- Vacuum pump (should the freeze dryer not have one built in)
- Freeze dryer trays
- Airtight bag or vacuum-sealed container

Making Salt Water Taffy:

- **Get ready Components:** Before you begin cooking, gather and measure all of the ingredients.
- Mix the sugar, butter, corn syrup, and water together: Put the unsalted butter, water, light corn syrup, and granulated sugar in a saucepan. Stir until the sugar melts over a medium heat source.
- **Cook to Soft Ball Stage:** Cook the mixture, stirring occasionally, until it reaches the soft ball stage, which is approximately 240°F/116°C. Insert a functioning candy thermometer into the mixture.
- Mix in the glycerin, salt, and cornstarch by dissolving it in a tiny quantity of water and adding it to the mixture. Add the salt and glycerin (if using) as well. Mix thoroughly.
- Taffy's flavor and color can be achieved by removing the mixture from the heat and adding food coloring and flavor extracts of your choosing. Mix thoroughly until fully incorporated.
- **Cool Slightly:** Until the combination is safe to handle, let it cool slightly.
- **Pull and Shape:** Using buttery hands, start pulling the taffy until it takes on a light tint and a satiny, silky consistency. Pull the taffy and form it into a rope.
- **Cut into Bite-Sized Pieces:** Using a butter knife, cut the taffy rope into little pieces.

➤ **Dust with Powdered Sugar:** To keep the taffy from sticking, dust each piece with powdered sugar.

The Freeze-Drying Method:

★ **Getting Ready for Freeze Drying:** Before freeze-drying, let the pieces of salt water taffy cool fully.

★ **How to Fill the Freeze Dryer:** In accordance with the manufacturer's recommendations, preheat the freeze dryer.

★ **Arrange the Taffy on Trays:** Place the chopped salt water taffy pieces in a uniform layer on the freeze-dryer trays.

★ **Establish Freeze Dryer Settings:** Aim for a low temperature of approximately -20°F to -40°F (-29°C to -40°C) for the freeze dryer, and follow the machine's instructions for adjusting the vacuum pressure.

★ **Start the Cycle of Freeze-Drying:** Begin the process of freeze-drying. The device will start the process of removing moisture from the saltwater taffy and progressively reduce the temperature.

★ **Keep an eye on the process:** Make sure to periodically monitor the freeze-drying cycle's progress. The time frame might be different, although it might take a day or two. As necessary, adjust the settings.

★ **Verify the Dryness:** Make sure the pieces of salt water taffy that have been freeze-dried are completely dry. Their texture need to be crisp and airy.

★ **Cool Down:** Before handling, let the salt water taffy that has been freeze-dried come to room temperature.

★ **Keep Safe:** To preserve their crispness, store the freeze-dried salt water taffy in an airtight receptacle or vacuum-sealed bag.

Advice and Adaptations:

- **Try Different Flavors:** To create a range of taffy possibilities, experiment with different flavor extracts like peppermint, vanilla, or fruit flavors.
- **Make a Colorful Rainbow:** To make a vibrant selection, divide the taffy mixture and add different food colors.
- **Add optional coconut or nuts:** To enhance texture and taste, mix in shredded coconut or chopped almonds.
- **Use Molds to Create Shaped Taffy (Optional):** Shape salt water taffy by using molds rather than cutting it into pieces.
- **Present Boxes:** For a charming homemade gift, present the freeze-dried salt water taffy in attractive bags or boxes.

29. Cotton CandyFlavored Treat

Components:

- 1 cup of sugar, granulated
- One-fourth cup water
- One-fourth cup corn syrup
- Half a teaspoon of flavoring for cotton candy
- One or two drops of optional pink or blue food coloring

Equipment:

- Cotton candy machine
- A candy thermometer
- Silicone matting or parchment paper
- The freezer dryer
- Vacuum pump (should the freeze dryer not have one built in)
- Freeze dryer trays
- Airtight bag or vacuum-sealed container

Cotton Candy Getting ready:

- ➢ **Get the cotton candy machine ready:** Install your cotton candy machine by following the directions provided by the manufacturer.
- ➢ **Make the Cotton Candy Concoction:** Put the corn syrup, water, and granulated sugar in a saucepan. Stir until the sugar melts over medium heat.
- ➢ **Boil and Check Temperature:** Using a candy thermometer, bring the mixture to a boil and simmer it until it reaches the hard crack stage, which is 160°C (320°F).

111

- ➤ **Incorporate Color and Flavor:** Take off the heat and mix in the flavoring for cotton candy. For added color, use food coloring.
- ➤ **Cool Slightly:** Make sure the mixture cools just enough to pourable consistency.
- ➤ **Cotton Candy Spinning:** Switch on your cotton candy maker. To enable the machine to gather the spun sugar, pour the flavored sugar mixture into the spinning head.
- ➤ **Collect Cotton Candy:** As the machine gathers the cotton candy, use a cone or stick to collect it. To gather extra cotton candy, twist the cone or wrap it around the bowl of the machine.
- ➤ **Serve Right Away:** Fresh cotton candy is best consumed, so serve it right away.
- ➤ **Keep Any Remaining Candies Stored:** To preserve texture, store any leftovers in an airtight container; however, keep in mind that cotton candy has a tendency to melt and become sticky with time.

The Freeze-Drying Method:
- ★ **Getting Ready for Freeze Drying:** After preparing the cotton candy, let it cool to room temperature before freezing it.
- ★ **How to Fill the Freeze Dryer:** In accordance with the manufacturer's recommendations, preheat the freeze dryer.
- ★ To ensure consistent freeze-drying, place the cotton candy on trays in the freezer and distribute it evenly.

★ **Establish Freeze Dryer Settings:** Aim for a low temperature of approximately -20°F to -40°F (-29°C to -40°C) for the freeze dryer, and follow the machine's instructions for adjusting the vacuum pressure.

★ **Start the Cycle of Freeze-Drying:** Begin the process of freeze-drying. The device will start to gently reduce the cotton candy's temperature and remove moisture from it.

★ **Keep an ye on the process:** Make sure to periodically monitor the freeze-drying cycle's progress. The time frame might be different, although it might take a day or two. As necessary, adjust the settings.

★ **Verify the Dryness:** Make sure the cotton candy that has been freeze-dried is completely dry. It need to be crisp in texture.

★ **Cool Down:** Before handling, let the cotton candy that has been freeze-dried come to room temperature.

★ **Take out of the trays:** The freeze-dried cotton candy should be carefully taken out of the pans.

★ **Keep Safe:** To keep the cotton candy crisp, store it in an airtight jar or vacuum-sealed bag once it has been freeze-dried.

Last Words of Advice:

● **Preference for Texture:** Depending on how you like your freeze-dried cotton candy to be crunchy or brittle, you can adjust the amount of time it freeze-dries.

- **Try It Out:** You may play about with the length of the freeze-drying process to get the right amount of crunch and taste for your cotton candy.
- **Storage:** Keep the cotton candy that has been freeze-dried in a dry, cool area. To keep its crisp texture, keep it away from dampness.

30. Grand Yogurt-Covered Treats
Components:
- Various sweets (such as biscuits, pretzels, almonds, or dried fruit)
- One cup of Greek or normal yogurt
- Two teaspoons (optional, for sweetness) of honey or maple syrup
- One teaspoon of optional vanilla essence (for flavor)

Equipment:
- Bowls for mixing
- Utensil or spatula
- Paper parchment
- Baking sheet
- The freezer dryer
- Vacuum pump (should the freeze dryer not have one built in)
- Freeze dryer trays
- Airtight bag or vacuum-sealed container

Treats Covered in Yogurt Getting ready:

> **Assemble the Ingredients:** Prepare a selection of candies that are ready to dip.

> **Assemble the yogurt coating:** Greek yogurt, vanilla extract, and honey or maple syrup (if used) should all be combined in a mixing dish. Mix thoroughly until fully incorporated. To suit your tastes, adjust the flavor and sweetness.

> **Dip Treats:** Make sure each treat is completely coated by dipping it into the yogurt mixture using a spoon or spatula.

> **Let Extra Yogurt Drip Off:** To ensure a thin and equal coating, let the extra yogurt mixture drip off the goodies.

> **Put this on parchment paper:** Place every coated treat on a baking sheet covered with parchment paper. Treats should not contact in order to avoid sticking.

> **Freeze for First Configuration (Optional):** Put the baking sheet in the freezer for ten to fifteen minutes to quickly set it. This promotes a quicker firming of the yogurt covering.

> **Double Dip (Optional):** After the first coating has solidified, repeat the dipping procedure for a thicker yogurt coating. If necessary, refreeze.

> **Freeze Until Solid:** Once completely covered, place the baking sheet in the freezer to allow the yogurt-covered candies to solidify. A few hours may pass for this.

How to Fill the Freeze Dryer:

★ **Set up the Freeze Dryer:** In accordance with the manufacturer's recommendations, preheat the freeze dryer.

★ **Place Candies on Trays:** Make sure the frozen yogurt-covered snacks are evenly spaced out on the freeze-dryer trays.

★ **Establish Freeze Dryer Settings:** Aim for a low temperature of approximately -20°F to -40°F (-29°C to -40°C) for the freeze dryer, and follow the machine's instructions for adjusting the vacuum pressure.

★ **Launch the Freeze-Dry Cycle:** Begin the process of freeze-drying. The yogurt-covered goodies will begin to lose moisture as the machine progressively lowers the temperature.

★ **Keep an eye on the process:** Make sure to periodically monitor the freeze-drying cycle's progress. The time frame might be different, although it might take a day or two. As necessary, adjust the settings.

★ **Verify the Dryness:** Make sure the snacks covered in freeze-dried yogurt are completely dry. They ought to be crisp in texture.

★ **Cool Down:** Before handling, let the freeze-dried snacks come to room temperature.

★ **Remove from Trays:** Gently take the goodies covered in freeze-dried yogurt out of the trays.

★ **Keep Safe:** To preserve their crispness, store the freeze-dried snacks in an airtight receptacle or vacuum-sealed bag.

Advice and Adaptations:

- **Try Different Treats:** For a wide range of freeze-dried yogurt-covered snacks, try a variety of goodies.
- **Adorn with garnishes:** For extra texture and taste, top the freeze-dried yogurt coating with chopped nuts, shredded coconut, or a drizzle of melted chocolate.
- **Custom Flavors:** Try a variety of yogurt flavors or add a little of zest from an orange for a special touch.
- **Thin Yogurt combination:** Add a small amount of milk to thin the yogurt combination if it's too thick and make it dip-worthy.
- **Serve Chilled:** It is ideal to consume these freeze-dried delights cold, straight out of the freezer.

BONUS SECTION: 7-DAYS FREEZE

CANDY CHECKLIST

BONUS SECTION
7-DAY FREEZE CANDY
CHECKLIST

FREEZE CANDY *Checklist*

MATERIALS NEEDED		TICK
CANDY SELECTION		☐
DRY ICE PROCUREMENT	**FREEZE DRYER SETUP**	☐
INSULATING COOLER & LINING MATERIAL	FREEZE DRYER SETTINGS	☐
CRUSHING TOOL & MESH STRAINER		☐
WORK SAFETY	**WORK SAFETY**	
GLOVES AND SAFETY GEAR	GLOVES AND SAFETY GEAR	☐
VENTILATION	VENTILATION	☐
PREPARATION	**CANDY PREPARATION**	
CANDY ARRANGEMENTS	CANDY ARRANGEMENTS	☐
COOLER SEALING	PRE-FREEZE	☐
MONITORING TIME	LOAD FREEZE DRYER & MONITORING	
MESH STRAINING	CHECK DRYNESS	☐
STORAGE CONTAINER	REMOVAL FROM FREEZE DRYER & STORAGE	☐

OBSERVATION

_____

_____

_____

_____

_____

_____

ADDITIONAL TIPS

_____

_____

_____

_____

_____

_____

FREEZE CANDY *Checklist*

MATERIALS NEEDED		TICK
CANDY SELECTION		☐
DRY ICE PROCUREMENT	FREEZE DRYER SETUP	☐
INSULATING COOLER & LINING MATERIAL	FREEZE DRYER SETTINGS	☐
CRUSHING TOOL & MESH STRAINER		☐
WORK SAFETY	WORK SAFETY	
GLOVES AND SAFETY GEAR	GLOVES AND SAFETY GEAR	☐
VENTILATION	VENTILATION	☐
PREPARATION	CANDY PREPARATION	
CANDY ARRANGEMENTS	CANDY ARRANGEMENTS	☐
COOLER SEALING	PRE-FREEZE	☐
MONITORING TIME	LOAD FREEZE DRYER & MONITORING	
MESH STRAINING	CHECK DRYNESS	☐
STORAGE CONTAINER	REMOVAL FROM FREEZE DRYER & STORAGE	☐

OBSERVATION

_____
_____
_____
_____
_____
_____

ADDITIONAL TIPS

_____
_____
_____
_____
_____
_____

FREEZE CANDY *Checklist*

MATERIALS NEEDED		TICK
CANDY SELECTION		☐
DRY ICE PROCUREMENT	**FREEZE DRYER SETUP**	☐
INSULATING COOLER & LINING MATERIAL	FREEZE DRYER SETTINGS	☐
CRUSHING TOOL & MESH STRAINER		☐
WORK SAFETY	**WORK SAFETY**	
GLOVES AND SAFETY GEAR	GLOVES AND SAFETY GEAR	☐
VENTILATION	VENTILATION	☐
PREPARATION	**CANDY PREPARATION**	
CANDY ARRANGEMENTS	CANDY ARRANGEMENTS	☐
COOLER SEALING	PRE-FREEZE	☐
MONITORING TIME	LOAD FREEZE DRYER & MONITORING	
MESH STRAINING	CHECK DRYNESS	☐
STORAGE CONTAINER	REMOVAL FROM FREEZE DRYER & STORAGE	☐

OBSERVATION

_____

_____

_____

_____

_____

_____

ADDITIONAL TIPS

_____

_____

_____

_____

_____

_____

FREEZE CANDY *Checklist*

MATERIALS NEEDED		TICK
CANDY SELECTION		☐
DRY ICE PROCUREMENT	FREEZE DRYER SETUP	☐
INSULATING COOLER & LINING MATERIAL	FREEZE DRYER SETTINGS	☐
CRUSHING TOOL & MESH STRAINER		☐
WORK SAFETY	**WORK SAFETY**	
GLOVES AND SAFETY GEAR	GLOVES AND SAFETY GEAR	☐
VENTILATION	VENTILATION	☐
PREPARATION	**CANDY PREPARATION**	
CANDY ARRANGEMENTS	CANDY ARRANGEMENTS	☐
COOLER SEALING	PRE-FREEZE	☐
MONITORING TIME	LOAD FREEZE DRYER & MONITORING	
MESH STRAINING	CHECK DRYNESS	☐
STORAGE CONTAINER	REMOVAL FROM FREEZE DRYER & STORAGE	☐

OBSERVATION

_____
_____
_____
_____
_____
_____
_____

ADDITIONAL TIPS

_____
_____
_____
_____
_____
_____
_____

FREEZE CANDY *Checklist*

MATERIALS NEEDED		TICK
CANDY SELECTION		☐
DRY ICE PROCUREMENT	**FREEZE DRYER SETUP**	☐
INSULATING COOLER & LINING MATERIAL	FREEZE DRYER SETTINGS	☐
CRUSHING TOOL & MESH STRAINER		☐
WORK SAFETY	**WORK SAFETY**	
GLOVES AND SAFETY GEAR	GLOVES AND SAFETY GEAR	☐
VENTILATION	VENTILATION	☐
PREPARATION	**CANDY PREPARATION**	
CANDY ARRANGEMENTS	CANDY ARRANGEMENTS	☐
COOLER SEALING	PRE-FREEZE	☐
MONITORING TIME	LOAD FREEZE DRYER & MONITORING	
MESH STRAINING	CHECK DRYNESS	☐
STORAGE CONTAINER	REMOVAL FROM FREEZE DRYER & STORAGE	☐

OBSERVATION

_____
_____
_____
_____
_____
_____

ADDITIONAL TIPS

_____
_____
_____
_____
_____
_____

FREEZE CANDY *Checklist*

MATERIALS NEEDED		TICK
CANDY SELECTION		☐
DRY ICE PROCUREMENT	**FREEZE DRYER SETUP**	☐
INSULATING COOLER & LINING MATERIAL	FREEZE DRYER SETTINGS	☐
CRUSHING TOOL & MESH STRAINER		☐
WORK SAFETY	**WORK SAFETY**	
GLOVES AND SAFETY GEAR	GLOVES AND SAFETY GEAR	☐
VENTILATION	VENTILATION	☐
PREPARATION	**CANDY PREPARATION**	
CANDY ARRANGEMENTS	CANDY ARRANGEMENTS	☐
COOLER SEALING	PRE-FREEZE	☐
MONITORING TIME	LOAD FREEZE DRYER & MONITORING	
MESH STRAINING	CHECK DRYNESS	☐
STORAGE CONTAINER	REMOVAL FROM FREEZE DRYER & STORAGE	☐

OBSERVATION

_____

_____

_____

_____

_____

_____

_____

ADDITIONAL TIPS

_____

_____

_____

_____

_____

_____

_____

FREEZE CANDY *Checklist*

MATERIALS NEEDED		TICK
CANDY SELECTION		☐
DRY ICE PROCUREMENT	**FREEZE DRYER SETUP**	☐
INSULATING COOLER & LINING MATERIAL	FREEZE DRYER SETTINGS	☐
CRUSHING TOOL & MESH STRAINER		☐
WORK SAFETY	**WORK SAFETY**	
GLOVES AND SAFETY GEAR	GLOVES AND SAFETY GEAR	☐
VENTILATION	VENTILATION	☐
PREPARATION	**CANDY PREPARATION**	
CANDY ARRANGEMENTS	CANDY ARRANGEMENTS	☐
COOLER SEALING	PRE-FREEZE	☐
MONITORING TIME	LOAD FREEZE DRYER & MONITORING	
MESH STRAINING	CHECK DRYNESS	☐
STORAGE CONTAINER	REMOVAL FROM FREEZE DRYER & STORAGE	☐

OBSERVATION

_____

_____

_____

_____

_____

_____

ADDITIONAL TIPS

_____

_____

_____

_____

_____

_____

Made in United States
Troutdale, OR
01/06/2025

27545080R10071